WALKING
—THE—
DARTMOOR
WAY

MICHAEL BENNIE

With illustrations by Jonathan Bennie

**Peninsula
Press**

First published in 2007 by Peninsula Press,
an imprint of Forest Publishing
Woodstock
Liverton
Newton Abbot
Devon TQ12 6JJ

British Library Cataloguing in Publication Data

A catalogue record for this book is available from the British Library.

ISBN 978-1-872640-54-9

Editorial, design and layout by:
Mike Lang

Front cover illustration by:
John W. Taylor

Typeset by:
Carnaby Typesetting, Torquay, Devon TQ1 1EG

Printed and bound in Great Britain by:
Cromwell Press Ltd, Trowbridge, Wiltshire BA14 0XB

Contents

Introduction

The Dartmoor Way is a circuit of the Dartmoor National Park of almost 140km/90 miles. It follows green lanes, farm paths, moorland tracks and quiet lanes through a beautifully varied landscape, including rolling farmland, deep wooded valleys, cascading streams, pretty villages and historic towns as well as the open spaces, panoramic views, strange-shaped tors and barren wastes of the moor itself.

In this book I have put together twenty-four circular walks that between them cover the whole of the Dartmoor Way. Each route links with the one before and the one that follows so that, if you wish, you can extend your walk by combining two legs of the Way. (I have indicated with an asterisk in the route descriptions where each stretch of the Dartmoor Way begins and ends.) They pass sites of historic or archaeological interest, areas of great natural beauty, and places which have become associated with the rich folklore of the moor.

The walks range in length from 6.5km/4 miles to 13km/8 miles; some are relatively easy, along clear paths with very little climbing, others are more challenging, with rougher terrain and several hills, some steep. But I have graded them so that you can see at a glance how difficult each is likely to be: A means that the route follows clear, easy paths with virtually no climbing of any significance; B means that the going will be slightly tougher, probably with one or two steady climbs and perhaps a bit of rough terrain; and routes marked C will have several steep hills and perhaps more rough terrain. I also give an indication of the approximate time each walk is likely to take. This is only a very rough approximation, however, since people will obviously walk at different speeds, and some may stop along the way to admire a particularly stunning view or explore an interesting site.

In addition to information on the length and time of each walk, there is advice on where to park if you are driving, but you may like to take advantage of the excellent bus services that link many of the starting points. I also give recommendations on where you might go for refreshment, usually before or after the walk but occasionally halfway round. On many of the routes there may only be one pub or restaurant, but in the larger centres there are likely to be several, and here I give my own preferences - but please be aware that the choices and their descriptions are purely personal.

There is a sketch map for each walk, but if you want to confirm the routes on an Ordnance Survey map you will find them all on Explorer OL28 Dartmoor, except for short stretches of Walks 20, 21 and 22 around North Brentor and Bridestowe, which are on Explorer 112 Launceston & Holsworthy, and parts of Walks 9 and 10, which are on Explorer 110 Torquay & Dawlish.

Finally a word of warning. Much of northern Dartmoor is part of one of the three military ranges, where live firing takes place from time to time. None of the routes in this book takes you onto the ranges, but Walks 21 and 24 take you close. If you are planning to extend either of those walks to take in some of the open moor, therefore, you should ring the telephone number given in the route summaries for those walks to find out whether firing is taking place in those areas. On no account should you venture onto the ranges (which are marked with red and white poles and noticeboards) when there are red flags flying from the nearby hills and tors.

Map showing the starting points of the walks

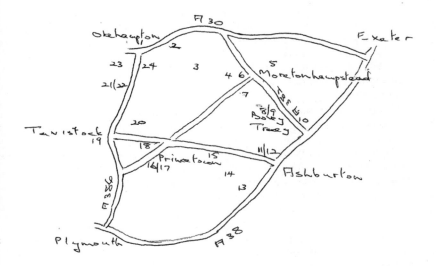

1. Okehampton to Sticklepath

Start and finish: Okehampton. Outside the Museum of Dartmoor Life in the courtyard to the right of the White Hart Hotel in West Street. Grid ref. 588951.

Parking: There are several car parks in Okehampton. The most convenient is off Market Street, which runs north opposite the hotel.

Length: 12km (7½ miles)

Approximate time: 4 hours

Degree of difficulty: C

Refreshments: There are several pubs and tearooms in Okehampton, but my choice is the White Hart Hotel. It is ideally situated for the start of the walk and is a delightful inn, full of character and history. William Pitt the elder, who was MP for Okehampton, held his celebration dinners there, and Emperor Haile Selassie of Ethiopia visited it during his exile in the 1930s. There are two low-beamed bars, one with an open fire, and the food ranges from sandwiches to main courses, including a wide vegetarian choice. If you want to stop halfway round, I would suggest either the tearoom at Finch Foundry (only open from March to October) or the Devonshire Inn, both in Sticklepath.

Route summary: This lovely stretch of the Dartmoor Way follows the East Okement and Taw Rivers through some of the most beautiful woodland in Devon - an area that features in Henry Williamson's classic book *Tarka the Otter*. It leaves the Way at the pretty village of Sticklepath and returns to Okehampton along green lanes, farm paths and another attractive wood. There are two museums to visit, one at each end of the Way.

You might like to visit the Museum of Dartmoor Life before setting off; it has a fascinating display on the life of ordinary moor folk over the centuries.

*To start the walk, follow the passageway that runs to the right of the museum and turn left into Jacob's Pool at the end. At the T-junction turn right and follow the road round to the left, past the entrances to Simmons Park and Okehampton Community College. Soon you will come to Town Mills, an eighteenth-century watermill. Climb the steps to the left of the mill and at the top turn right. You will see a footpath sign for Ball Hill; follow the road past the college to a gate. Continue along the surfaced path on the other side. You go through a succession of gates, following the leat for Town Mills, finally joining the river and emerging onto a lane. Turn left (signposted to Exeter Road). At the junction go straight on and then immediately right (signposted to Tordown). Go under a railway line and then the A30 dual carriageway.

About 250 metres beyond the A30 turn right through a gate, following the public footpath sign for the road near Cleave House. Cross a small clapper bridge and follow the field boundary on the other side round to the right.

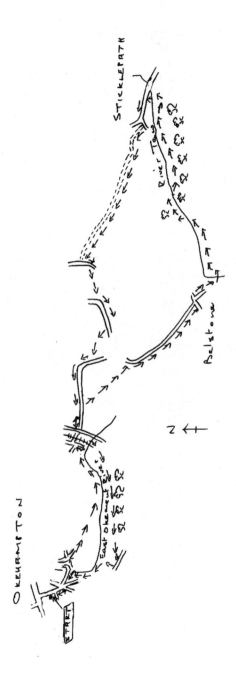

Cross a stile and keep to the right of the next field. You climb steeply, but at the top you get a good view back over the rolling countryside. Cross a stile and keep to the left of the next field to a gate. Bear left and cross another field to a stile into a lane; turn right. Follow this lane for almost 1km/²/₃ mile to Belstone. At the T-junction in the village go left and then immediately right. Pass the Tors Inn and when you come to the green on the edge of the village, cut across it to a track leading down to the valley.

It swings left and then right to a footbridge. On the other side go left and follow the path which follows the line of the river. After some distance there is a fork; go left down to the river and then alongside it. You will eventually come to a footbridge on your left; cross over into Skaigh Wood and turn right.

THE RIVER TAW, SKAIGH WOOD

After about 300 metres you will find a signpost pointing right; follow it down to the river again and cross another footbridge. It is beautiful along here, as the path hugs the river, with a mass of rhododendrons lining the path. It was here that Tarka the Otter fought over a rabbit with a band of stoats in Henry Williamson's classic.

The path follows the river for about 1.25km/³/₄ mile and broadens to a track. At the T-junction turn left (signposted to Sticklepath and the A30). Go through a gate and after a short distance turn left across the river, following the sign for the Museum of Water Power. This brings you out at Finch Foundry, a working nineteenth-century water-powered forge owned by the National Trust. Follow the drive through an archway into the main road.*

Turn left to follow the road out of the village. On the outskirts, as the road bends to the right, turn left (signposted to Skaigh) and immediately right up a rough track, following the bridlepath sign for Tongue End and Skaigh. You come to realise why the village is called Sticklepath ('stickle' is an old word for 'steep') as the track climbs up the side of the Taw valley. When you come to a house, swing left to a gate. There is a superb view of the moor over the wall on the left, with Yes Tor prominent on the horizon. About 500 metres after joining the track you come to a junction; go straight on (signposted to Tongue End). After another 500 metres there is another junction; go straight on again. After a while there is another very good view to your right.

You emerge onto a lane; turn left and after about 100 metres look for a stile on the right. There is a sign pointing to Lower Priestacott, but it is not easy to see. Bear left across a field to a gap in a bank. Cut straight across the next field to a gate and then bear slightly right to a stile into another lane; turn left. After 500 metres you will see a sign pointing through a gate to the road near Eastlake; turn off here and go diagonally left across a field to a stile in the corner. Follow the hedge on the other side and, when it goes right, cut straight across to a gate, and across the next field to a stile. Turn right in the lane beyond.

Follow this lane as it swings left and then goes under the A30 and a railway line. You are now temporarily on the route you came out on. At the T-junction turn left and at the next junction go left again, following the footpath signs. Where the path you came out on branches right, go straight on and through a gate. Go under the railway line again and cross a tributary of the East Okement River. Turn right and cross the East Okement itself, and then turn right again on the other side (signposted to Station Road). Cross a stile and continue along a track on the other side into a wood. The track runs parallel to the river but a little distance away from (and a bit later above) it. On the outskirts of Okehampton go through a gate onto an unsurfaced lane. You come out at a road; turn right and then almost immediately right again on a path signposted to the town centre via Simmons Park.

At the path junction go sharp left, following the signpost for the town centre direct. At each of the forks in the path keep left, alongside a wall. You reach a road and leave Simmons Park. When you come to a T-junction turn right and after a short distance left into Jacob's Pool. The Museum of Dartmoor Life is down on the right.

2. Sticklepath to Wonson

Start and finish: Sticklepath. Outside Finch Foundry in the main street through the village. Grid ref. 642941.

Parking: In the main street.

Length: 13km (8 miles)

Approximate time: $4^1/2$ hours

Degree of difficulty: C

Refreshments: You are spoilt for choice on this leg of the Way. There are two pubs in Sticklepath, as well as the tearoom at the National Trust's Finch Foundry (only open from March to October). At South Zeal, shortly after the start, there are another two pubs, and if you want a break in the middle of the walk, try the Northmore Arms in Wonson. My choice would be the Devonshire Inn in Sticklepath, an Elizabethan building which retains its charm and offers snack lunches.

Route summary: You follow the Dartmoor Way along lanes and farm paths through the delightful villages of South Zeal and Throwleigh and then take a pretty green lane to Wonson, with some good views along the way. The return leg takes you over the open moor, where the views will take your breath away, and back to Sticklepath via a network of walled tracks and the lovely Skaigh Wood. There are some stiff climbs and a few wet and muddy patches, but the views are worth the effort. **Note:** Navigation across the moorland stretch is relatively easy in clear weather, but you should not attempt it in poor visibility unless you are confident in the use of map and compass. An alternative route is given, which avoids the open moor (but also misses the best of the views).

---

*Turn east along the road through Sticklepath (right from Finch Foundry) and follow it through the village. Cross the River Taw and on the other side turn left up a lane. It climbs quite steeply and at the top you get a good view of the moor on your right before dipping down to South Zeal. Go through the village, passing a lane going right to a car park, and climb out the other side. Take the next lane on the right, near the top, and continue climbing. It comes out at a main road; cross over to another lane and after a few metres turn right onto a path leading into a thicket. You come out onto Ramsley Hill, with a good view of the moor ahead of you.

Around you are the remains of the Ramsley copper mine, with the chimney on the hill to your left. Although tin was the mainstay of the economy of the high moor, here on the edge a number of other minerals were mined, including copper. Ramsley was a copper mine, and operated between the 1850s and 1909. There is a viewing platform on the right, with a superb view over South Zeal, with Exmoor in the distance. As you continue round the hill you will see the spoil heaps from the mine; go to the right of the large one and you will find the path descending to a road; bear left.

After 600 metres you will come to a junction; go straight on (signposted to Throwleigh and Gidleigh). You now get a good view of the moor to the right. You cross Blackaton Brook and then a cattle grid. At the junction just beyond the cattle grid go straight on (signposted to Throwleigh). You now get another good view across the farmland on your left. Cross another cattle grid and you start to descend. Then, after about 200 metres, as the lane bends to the left, turn right through a gate, following the public footpath sign to Throwleigh village.

Keep to the right of the field beyond to a stile. Keep to the right again to reach a gate on the right. Bear left across the next field. The ground can be rather boggy, but it is quite passable. At the end cross a stile and then a stream. You emerge into a field; go diagonally right, aiming for the church. Cross another stile and cut across to the left to a kissing-gate leading into Throwleigh churchyard. Pass the church and go through the lych-gate into a lane. Turn right and climb out of the village. After about 100 metres turn left up the drive of a house called The Hey. When it swings left, turn right up a sunken green lane (signposted 'Byway to Wonson'). Follow this pretty lane

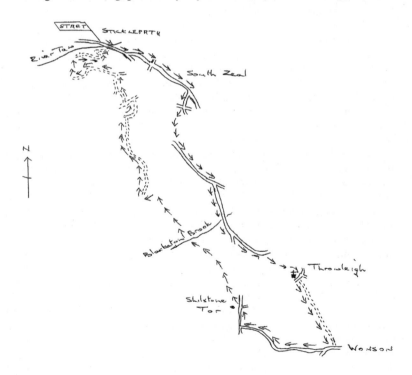

THE LYCH-GATE,
THROWLEIGH

(which can become muddy at times) for a little over 1km/³/₄ mile and you will emerge onto a lane just outside the hamlet of Wonson.*

Turn left to continue along the Dartmoor Way and then left again if you want to make a detour to the Northmore Arms. Otherwise, to continue this walk, turn right and after 200 metres right again (signposted to Ash). The lane crosses a cattle grid and winds through the gorse to a T-junction; turn right (signposted to Throwleigh). At the next junction go straight on (signposted to South Zeal). Just beyond you will see Shilstone Tor on the left, with paths going off around it. Bear left along the lowest one. (If visibility is poor or you are concerned about your navigation over the open moor, you can carry on along the road and rejoin the main route further on.)

The path runs below the tor, and as it climbs you get a magnificent view over to your right. Where it forks, go left up the hill. It becomes less distinct as it climbs, and the gorse becomes thicker, but if you pick your way through, keeping roughly to your initial direction, you should be all right - aim for the dead tree you can see ahead of you. Soon you can enjoy the most stunning 180-degree panorama behind you over the moor and the surrounding farmland. As you ascend, you will see a large hill on the horizon; aim to the right of that. Then, as you come over the crest of the hill, a wall becomes visible stretching up the opposite hillside to your right; that is where you want to be. You go down a steep hill to Blackaton Brook; find somewhere to cross near Shilley Pool and follow the wall on the other side. (If you have chosen the road route, you should follow it for 1.2km/³/₄ mile from Shilstone Tor to a junction and bear left. Take a bridlepath on the left about 300 metres further on, and that will bring you out onto the moor towards Shilley Pool.)

When the wall peters out, keep straight on to another one. You continue to enjoy lovely views to the right. When the new wall bends to the right, you will see another one ahead of you. Follow it up the hill and at the corner go round to join a track that runs alongside it. Soon another wall comes in from the left; follow the track between the two. It can be very wet along this stretch so take care. It descends to a gate and continues for some distance to a T-junction; turn right, go through another gate and follow the track to the left. At the next junction go straight on (signposted to the A30 at Prospect). At the next T-junction go left and after 200 metres right (signposted to Ford Cross and the A30). When you come to the gate to Beacon Cottage bear right along a green lane. You come out at another track; bear right.

This track emerges onto a surfaced lane; turn left. Cross a stream and go straight on along a track that climbs steadily. You go through a gate and follow the track to the left and right. Go through another gate at the top and after a few metres turn right through another gate, following the public bridlepath sign. You get an excellent view ahead of you. Keep to the right of a field and when you come to a gate bear left just before it to follow the edge of the field down. At the bottom turn right through a gate to skirt the top of the lovely Skaigh Wood. After a while the track swings sharp left and at the bottom joins another track; turn right. Go through a gate and after a short distance go left across a footbridge (signposted to the Museum of Water Power). Follow the path on the other side to a gate into the Finch Foundry car park; turn right through another gate and follow a path to the foundry's drive. Turn right and go through an archway into the main street.

3. Wonson to Chagford

Start and finish: Wonson. Grid ref. 673896. However, if you are approaching from the south, Wonson is quite complicated to get to, so you might like to start in Chagford and do the second half of the route first.

Parking: There is parking alongside the road, especially alongside the telephone box at the top of Wonson. If you are starting in Chagford, there is a pay-and-display car park on the eastern edge of the town, just beyond the church.

Length: 11km (6³/₄ miles)

Approximate time: 3¹/₂ hours

Degree of difficulty: B

Refreshments: The Northmore Arms, in Wonson, is a charming pub. Some 400 years old, it consists of two small rooms, both with welcoming open fires in winter, and a small beer garden. The thick stone walls and small windows give it a warm, cosy atmosphere. There is a range of good home-made pub fare on offer. If you would like a break halfway round the route, there is a choice of three pubs and a café/delicatessen in Chagford.

Route summary: Lush green woods and cascading rivers and streams are the main attractions of this walk, linked by a succession of quiet lanes and pretty, ancient tracks. The outward leg follows the Dartmoor Way down to the valley of the River Teign, and you return via the delightful woods that flank the North Teign and the pretty village of Gidleigh.

---

*At the telephone box at the T-junction just above the Northmore Arms turn left (signposted to Chagford and Providence). After 400 metres/¹/₄ mile you pass Providence Chapel on the left and Providence Place on the right. Turn right along a green lane just beyond the latter (signposted to Coombe). Follow this pretty track and at the end go through a gate onto a surfaced drive. This takes you to a lane; turn left and follow it alongside a stream. Cross a bridge and follow the lane round to the left. Cross another two bridges in quick succession and immediately after the second turn right across a stile into Blackaton Wood. The path runs through the wood alongside Blackaton Brook for about 400 metres/¹/₄ mile and emerges via a stile into a lane; turn left.

Follow this lane to the hamlet of Murchington. At the first junction go straight on (signposted to Chagford). At the next junction bear right (signposted to Chagford again). At the top of the hill turn right across a stile. Keep to the right of a field and at the bottom cross another stile into a wood. Cross some stepping stones and follow the path above the River Teign. It swings left and ends at a stile leading into a lane; turn right. Cross Chagford Bridge and after 100 metres you will come to a crossroads. Turn left to visit Chagford or to continue along the Dartmoor Way. Otherwise, to continue this walk, turn right (signposted to Holy Street and Leigh Bridge).*

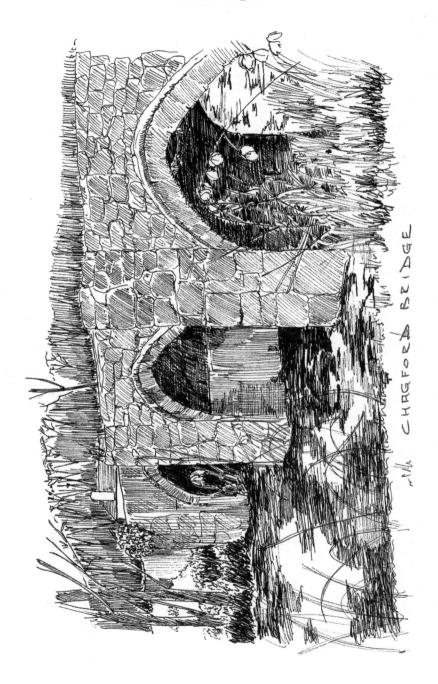

CHAGFORD BRIDGE

Follow the lane with a leat on your right and the Teign just beyond it. You pass the pretty Holystreet Manor and start climbing. After about 800 metres/¹/₂ mile you cross the South Teign River just above where it meets the North Teign and becomes the Teign. Just beyond the bridge, where the lane goes right to the Gidleigh Park Hotel, go straight on along a green lane marked 'Unsuitable for motors'. Climb some more, winding to the left and to the right. You come out onto a surfaced drive; go straight on, with a very good view to Meldon Hill to the left. Where the drive joins a lane, go straight on again.

You pass Teigncombe Manor on your left and, when the lane swings sharp right, go straight on along a track. After a short distance you come to a green lane on the right, signposted as a bridlepath to Kestor and footpath to Gidleigh. Turn right and climb up this pretty track for 150 metres to a junction; turn right (signposted to Gidleigh). You now get a lovely view to the right over the farms and woods. Go through a gate at the end onto a lane. Go left and then almost immediately right to cross a stile, and follow a track down to a conifer wood. Swing right to skirt along the top of the wood. You can hear the North Teign River below you on the left and soon you turn left to go down to meet it.

It is quite idyllic at the bottom, with the river cascading over large boulders and the woods all around. You may even be lucky enough to see some deer. Cross a footbridge and follow the path on the other side to a track; turn right. After 100 metres or so go left, following the path sign, and climb

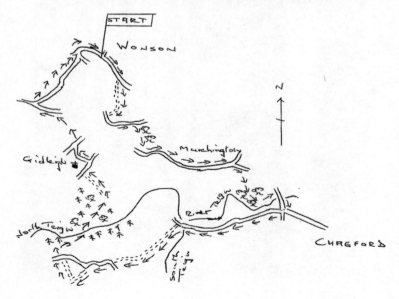

16

through the trees. At the top you join a track and get another excellent view half-right. At the end cross a stile into a lane and turn right. After 150 metres turn left (signposted to Gidleigh and Chapple). Pass the church and continue to a T-junction. Cross over to a footpath (signposted as the Mariners' Way to the road near Moortown).

Go straight across a field to a stake with a yellow footpath waymark on it and then to a gate. It can be rather muddy along this stretch after rain. Keep to the left on the other side to another gate and then keep to the left again to reach a third gate. Bear left on the other side and after a short distance you will come to a little clapper bridge across a stream on the right. Cross over and follow the path on the other side to a gate onto a lane; bear left. After 200 metres you come to a T-junction; turn right. After another 800 metres/^{1}/$_2$ mile there is another junction; go straight on (signposted to Wonson and Throwleigh). At the next junction go straight on again (signposted to Wonson and Throwleigh again). The phone box is about 300 metres further on.

4. Chagford to Fingle Bridge

Start and finish: Chagford. Grid ref. 701874.
Parking: There is a pay-and-display car park on the eastern edge of the town, just beyond the church.
Length: 12.5km (7³/₄ miles)
Approximate time: 4¹/₂ hours
Degree of difficulty: B
Refreshments: There are three pubs and a café/delicatessen in Chagford. I particularly like the Ring o' Bells, a delightful, atmospheric hostelry facing onto The Square, where the stannary court used to be held. It has a long bar in the front, divided into little alcoves by partitions and screens, and an attractively furnished dining area at the back. Behind the pub is a pretty courtyard with flower beds and an arbour. If you want a break halfway along the route, the Fingle Bridge Inn at Fingle Bridge is another lovely pub.
Route summary: Chagford is an ancient stannary town, where miners brought their tin to be assessed and weighed, and where offenders against the miners' laws were tried. It is a very pretty little town, and this route starts with a wander through its narrow streets. You then follow the banks of the River Teign for 4km/2¹/₂ miles, across fields and through woods, to the beautiful Fingle Bridge. There you leave the Dartmoor Way and climb high above the Teign, with magnificent views up the gorge to Dartmoor (and a chance via a short detour to visit the National Trust property of Castle Drogo), returning to Chagford along pretty, hedge-fringed lanes. It is all easy going, apart from one very steep climb halfway round.

Turn left as you leave the car park and return to the centre of Chagford. *When you reach The Square, turn right and follow the road out of the town. On the outskirts you pass a school; a little way beyond it turn left (signposted to the swimming pool). You cross the River Teign and soon come to the swimming pool. Just beyond it is Rushford Mill Farm; turn right here and cross the farmyard. At the path junction go straight on rather than right across a ford. Cross a stile into a field and keep alongside the river. It is lovely along here, with the sun on the river as it flows noisily along beside you.

At the end of the field go through a gate into a pretty wood. Look to your right and you will see an interesting sculpture on an island in the river. After 500 metres the path forks; bear right (signposted to Dogmarsh Bridge). Cross a wooden footbridge and go up some steps to a road. Cross to a kissing-gate and enter the Castle Drogo estate, following the sign for Fingle Bridge, Drewsteignton and Castle Drogo. Follow the river and, as you proceed, you will see Castle Drogo half left, perched on its promontory high above the valley. Despite its name, it is actually a country house rather than a castle.

'GRANITE SONG' SCULPTURE,
RIVER TEIGN

Designed by Sir Edwin Lutyens, it was built between 1911 and 1930 for Julius Drewe and is now owned by the National Trust.

Ignore the footbridge across the river on the right and carry on along the left bank. At the end of the field go through a kissing-gate. There is another kissing-gate at the end of the next field, although at the time of writing there was no fence alongside it. A final kissing-gate leads you into another wood. Ignore the rather splendid footbridge on your right and follow the path along the river bank, with the beautiful wood stretching up on your left and birdsong all around. The path climbs up the valley side from time to time and you go through one gate along the way, but essentially you follow the river bank for 2.4km/1½ miles until you emerge onto a lane opposite the Fingle Bridge Inn.*

Turn left and follow the lane for about 150 metres, then turn sharp left onto a path (signposted to the Hunter's Path, the road near Castle Drogo, and Drewsteignton). The path climbs steeply up the side of the valley and then swings right, continuing to climb through the wood, but more steadily now. After about 500 metres of climbing the path levels off and you emerge from the trees, to be rewarded for your efforts by a magnificent view up the Teign gorge to Dartmoor. Go through a gate and at the path junction go straight on (signposted to the road near Drogo and the Fisherman's Path). You pass two paths going up to Castle Drogo if you want to make a detour to visit it. Eventually, after just over 2km/1¼ miles, the path swings right round the promontory and descends to a gate onto a surfaced drive; bear right (signposted to the county road near Castle Drogo). When the drive joins a lane, turn left.

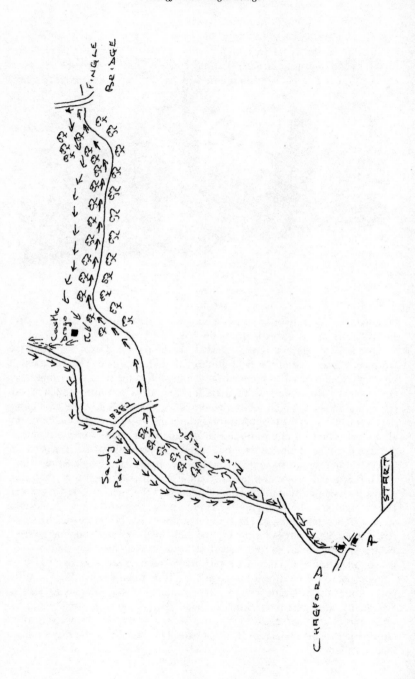

Follow this lane for 1.2km/³/₄ mile to a road. Cross to another lane (signposted to the swimming pool). After another 1.2km/³/₄ mile you pass Rushford Mill Farm again, and then the swimming pool. Follow the lane back to Chagford and at the T-junction turn right. At The Square turn left to return to the car park.

――――5. Fingle Bridge to Moretonhampstead――――

Start and finish: Fingle Bridge. Grid ref. 743899.
Parking: There is a free public car park across the bridge from the Fingle Bridge Inn. Please do not park alongside the lane leading to the bridge, as that is reserved for pub customers.
Length: 11.5km (7 miles)
Approximate time: 4 hours
Degree of difficulty: C
Refreshments: The Fingle Bridge Inn is a lovely spot. There is a large bar with two big granite fireplaces and a beamed ceiling. The place to be on a fine day, however, is on the terrace overlooking the river - it is quite idyllic, and you may decide to forgo the walk and just enjoy the view! The food is wideranging and tasty. If you want a break in the middle of your walk, Moretonhampstead has three pubs, a hotel and a tearoom.
Route summary: This is a walk of superb views and open moorland, but also pretty riverside paths and cool woodland. The outward leg follows the Dartmoor Way past an Iron Age hill fort to the pretty village of Moretonhampstead, and you return across the gorse-covered Mardon Down. Although navigation is not a problem, there are some rather muddy stretches and some very steep climbs to negotiate, hence its classification as C.

---

*From the car park, go back towards the bridge and just before you get to it turn sharp left up a track (signposted to Cranbrook Castle). It is a long and steep climb through the wood, so take it gently. Pause for a good view back across the valley. Near the top you will come to a finger-post. If you bear left along here (signposted to Moreton), you will save about 200 metres but miss the chance of visiting the Iron Age hill fort of Cranbrook Castle. If you want to visit the site, carry on up the track. After 250 metres you will see a path signposted right to Cranbrook Castle. The hill fort is in a superb defensive position, with extensive views all around and a very steep climb up from the valley to the north, but for some reason it was never completed. However, enough of the ramparts were built and still remain to enable one to imagine what it must have been like when first built, and the views to both the north and the south are superb.

Retrace your steps to the track and turn right. After a few metres you will come to a lane; turn left. Just beyond a farm, after 300 metres, turn right across a stile (signposted to Butterdon for Moreton). Keep to the right of a field and go through a gate. Keep to the right again and cross a stile; keep to the right yet again on the other side. At the end of the next field cross two stiles and bear right to follow the field boundary. You now get a lovely view across Dartmoor, with Haytor on the horizon. At the end of the next field follow the wall round to the left (signposted to the road near Butterdon). Go through a gate and follow a track round to join a drive. At the path junction go straight on (signposted to the county road and Willingstone). At the end turn right along a lane.

After 200 metres, as the lane turns right, go straight on along a track. Pass some cottages and, when the track ends, go straight on along a green lane. This takes you down through a wood to a gate. Continue along the path on the other side, which can be wet. You follow a pretty stream for a while and then veer away from it. You leave the wood and keep to the left of a field. Go through a gate on the left at the end and cross to another gate; bear left across the next field (signposted to Millbrook Bridge and Lime Street). Go through a gap in the bank in the far corner. You soon meet up with the stream again and go through a gate, and after a short distance cross a footbridge on the left. Turn right on the other side and follow the stream to a gate into a lane. Turn right and follow the lane into Moretonhampstead.*

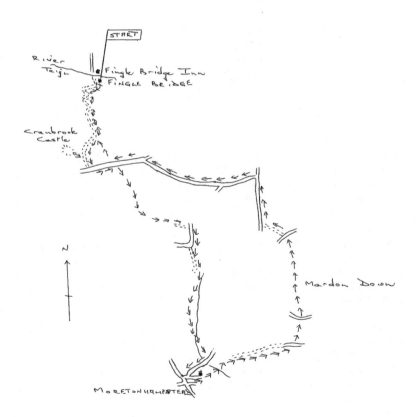

At the T-junction near the centre of this attractive village turn left along Fore Street, and at the end go into the churchyard. Go to the right of the church and through a gate at the end into a children's playground. Keep to the left to a kissing-gate and keep to the left of the field beyond, going down a steep hill. Cross a stile at the bottom and keep to the left again, following the sign to Yarningdale for Mardon. At the end go through another kissing-gate and up to a track; turn right and the track becomes a path. Cross a stile and keep to the right of another field alongside a stream, climbing as you go. Cross another stile and continue climbing up this very pretty path. You come out at a track by a farmyard; take the second path on the right (signposted to Yarningdale for Mardon again). Just beyond the farmyard, cross a stile into a green lane; it can be muddy along here as well. Pause at the top for a good view back over Moretonhampstead to the moor.

Go through a gate onto a track and go straight on (signposted to the path for Mardon). You come out onto a lane; go straight on. After 150 metres you will see a gap on the left leading to a gate and a path. There is no finger-post, but the gate is marked as a bridlepath to the moor. The views back and to the left as you follow this path (which can also be muddy) improve as you climb. You emerge through another gate onto Mardon Down; stop for a while here to admire the magnificent view back over the moor. Climb straight on up the down, crossing a road on the way. Do not worry too much about your precise route - you can always correct for any slight navigational errors later.

When you come to the top of the down, another superb view opens up ahead, and you now have an almost 360-degree panorama. You pass some ancient cairns along the way, and go down the other side of the down to a road. Turn left and after a short distance you will see a track on the right marked 'Farm access only'; turn down there. At the road at the end turn right. After 700 metres turn left (signposted to Chagford). At the next junction follow the main lane round to the right, and at the next go straight on (signposted to Chagford). About 400 metres after this junction look out for a gate and stile on the right just beyond the farm, with a signpost pointing to Fingle Bridge. If you took the slightly shorter route out, you are now on the same path again. Keep to the right of a field and go through a stone gateway at the end. Keep to the right again and towards the end you will find a stile on the right leading into a wood. Go through and follow the path to a track. This is the track you came out on; follow it down the hill through the wood to the car park.

——6. Moretonhampstead to North Bovey ——

Start and finish: Moretonhampstead. Grid ref. 753860.
Parking: There are two car parks in Moretonhampstead.
Length: 6.5km (4 miles)
Approximate time: 2 hours
Degree of difficulty: A
Refreshments: There are three pubs, a hotel and a tearoom in Moreton-hampstead. I particularly like the White Hart Hotel, which stands on the corner in the centre of the village. It is an old coaching inn, and is full of character. During the Napoleonic Wars it served as a meeting place for French officer prisoners of war on parole from Dartmoor Prison. In addition to the welcoming bar and restaurant, there is a pretty courtyard at the back. There is a mouth-watering array of food on offer, from sandwiches to soup and main courses. For a break in the middle of the walk try the Ring of Bells in North Bovey.
Route summary: The Dartmoor Way goes through the centre of Moreton-hampstead, a pretty, bustling village. It then follows farm paths and green lanes to the lovely thatched village of North Bovey. The return leg takes you along more farm paths and green lanes, with a quiet lane to finish off with. There are some excellent views along the way as well as a wealth of wild flowers in the hedges.

---

* Starting at the crossroads in the centre of Moretonhampstead, outside the White Hart, follow Court Street, the street that leads west, towards Princetown. Continue until you leave the village. Then, about 600 metres after setting off, look for a public footpath sign on the left for North Bovey (Beelands Lane). Follow it into a pretty green lane stretching down into a valley. It can become a little muddy in patches at times. Cross Wadley Brook at the bottom and follow a small tributary for a short while to two stiles in quick succession. Bear left in the field on the other side to a corner, where there is a yellow waymark and a signpost. Follow the left-hand field boundary to a gate. As you go, you get a good view to the left over Moreton-hampstead.

Go through a gate at the top and cut straight across the next field to another gate. This leads into a surfaced drive; turn left and after a few metres right through another gate, following the footpath sign. Keep to the right of a field and go through a gate. Cross the next field to a stile and keep to the right of another field. At the end a gate takes you onto a green lane; follow that to a lane. Turn right and almost immediately left to cross a stile. There is a signpost, but it is hidden by a bush. However, the stile is marked by a waymark. Go diagonally left across a field to the far corner, where there is a gate. Go through and after a few metres turn right through another gate, followed quickly by a third. Bear left across the field beyond to a stile in the middle of the fence. Go diagonally right across another field to a stile in the corner. Cross it into a lane. Turn left and as you follow the lane look to your right over the bank for a good view of the moor. At the T-junction turn right into North Bovey.

When you come to a junction just inside the village, bear left and pass the village green on your right. It is a delightful little village of stone and thatched cottages. Pass the entrance to the Ring of Bells and continue out of North Bovey to a gate. Continue along the track on the other side. After about 250 metres you will see a public footpath sign on the left; follow it across a stile into a green lane. *

At the top, just before you come to two gates, you will see a little path going left; follow it round to the right and over a stile into a field. Keep to the right and cross a stile at the end of the field. Go straight across the next field to another stile and a stream. Cross the next field, with a very good view on the right to Lustleigh Cleave and beyond. At the far corner go left through a gate and cross another field to a stile. Cross the next field to a gate on the

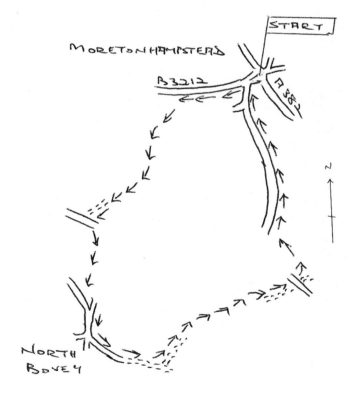

27

THE VILLAGE PUMP,
NORTH BOVEY

right; cross a concrete track and a stile on the other side. Yet another stile on the other side of the next field takes you into a green lane; turn left.

After 400 metres/¹/₄ mile you go through a gate onto a lane; cross over to a drive. After a few metres, as the drive swings right, go straight on to a stile and bear right across a field to another stile in the far corner. Keep to the right of the next two fields and go through a kissing-gate onto a track; cross it to another stile and keep to the right across two more fields. At the end of the second, cross a small stream and bear right. After a short distance one more stile takes you onto a lane; turn right. Follow the lane for 800 metres/¹/₂ mile to a T-junction on the edge of Moretonhampstead; turn right and at the top turn right again into Court Street.

7. North Bovey to Water

Start and finish: North Bovey. Grid ref. 739838.
Parking: There is a free car park on the southern edge of the village.
Length: 11km (6³/₄ miles)
Approximate time: 3¹/₂ hours
Degree of difficulty: C
Refreshments: The Ring of Bells in North Bovey is a delightful thatched pub set back from the village green. It has a small bar, with a lounge off it, and a separate restaurant. The food is delicious and ranges from soup and baguettes to a variety of main courses. If you would like a break near the middle of the walk, a short detour at Water will take you to the Kestor Inn.
Route summary: The Bovey valley woods, a national nature reserve, are the main feature of this lovely walk. The Dartmoor Way takes you along lanes, tracks and green lanes to the valley and the pretty hamlet of Water. The return leg is along the spectacular Lustleigh Cleave and another green lane. There are a few steep climbs along the way, especially up to the Cleave, and some wet and muddy stretches. But the attractions of the route far outweigh these disadvantages.

Turn right from the car park into North Bovey, and after a few metres turn right again past the green. * At the T-junction turn right again to follow a lane out of the village. Go through a gate at the end onto a track. Follow this, ignoring the paths and byways going off it. You descend to Dickford Bridge and then climb steadily on the other side, with a good view to the right to Easdon Down and then down the Bovey valley. After a while you will see the distinctive outline of Haytor on the horizon.

After some time the track becomes a surfaced lane again, and some 1.8km/1 mile after setting out you come to a T-junction; turn right. After a while the lane descends to the River Bovey and you can see Hunter's Tor at the top of Lustleigh Cleave. At the bottom you cross two stone bridges and then climb out of the valley again. After about 400 metres/¹/₄ mile there is a junction; go left (signposted to Manaton). This lane climbs gently and after another 400 metres/¹/₄ mile swings sharp right. As it does so, go straight on along a concrete track, following the signs for Horsham for the county road near Manaton and for Foxworthy Bridge.

After 100 metres or so, as the track bends left, bear right up a broad path (signposted to Horsham Steps or Manaton via Horsham). Be careful to take the right path, as the direction of the signpost is not very clear: do not turn sharp right, but half right along the broader path. As you get to the top, look left for a good view of Lustleigh Cleave and Hunter's Tor. The path narrows and continues to climb, then runs along the top of a wood. At the junction go straight on (signposted to Horsham for Water). Cross a stile and keep to the

A GOOSE HOUSE AND STEPS, NEADON

left of a long field, following the waymarked posts. As you go you get a good view ahead of you to Haytor Down. Cross another stile and keep to the left again to a gap in a bank. Follow a path on the other side alongside a track; do not follow the track itself, as it is likely to take you in the wrong direction. Yellow waymarks show you the way down to a gate alongside a house.

Go straight on on the other side (signposted to Manaton and Water). Pass the house and swing right along a track. After a few metres there is another junction; go straight on (signposted to Water). This is a pretty green lane edged by old granite walls. It broadens out into a track and enters a conifer plantation. When the conifers give way to more mixed woodland, look left for a good view across the valley. You finally emerge at a junction; the Dartmoor Way goes right, and you can turn off here for a short detour of a few hundred metres to the Kestor Inn if you wish. Otherwise turn left (signposted to the Bovey valley for Lustleigh). *

You are now following another pretty green lane, which runs downhill. After a few metres it forks; go left, following the footpath sign. It is rather wet along here, as there is a small rivulet running down the path. Go through a gate and continue down quite steeply through the beautiful wood, still with wet patches along the path. Towards the bottom you come to a junction; go straight on (signposted to Clam Bridge for Lustleigh Cleave). When you get down to the River Bovey there is another junction; go straight on across a log bridge (signposted to Hammerslake).

Follow the path as it climbs through the trees on the other side. After 400 metres/¹/₄ mile there is another junction; go left (signposted to Lustleigh via Hammerslake). This path climbs steeply, straight up the hill. At the next junction go left, straight up the hill again. After 100 metres or so, look out for a path going left; there is a signpost pointing to Foxworthy, but at the time of writing it is broken. You cross a muddy patch and continue along the side of Lustleigh Cleave. After a little over 800 metres/¹/₂ mile the path swings left and begins to descend. At the bottom is a junction; go straight on (signposted to Foxworthy).

Go through a gate and onto a drive; bear right, following the bridlepath sign. At the T-junction, after a couple of hundred metres, turn right (signposted to Peck Farm and the road near Barnecourt). Follow the track to some cottages; bear left and at the fork go right through a gate onto a green lane, following the direction of the blue arrow on the gatepost. Climb steeply up the green lane and, when you reach the top, look to the left for a good view of Easdon Down, with North Bovey visible half left. Go through a gate. After

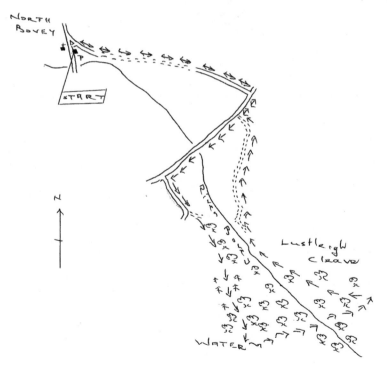

a while another gate takes you onto a concrete drive; bear left (signposted to the county road near Barnecourt).

After 400 metres/^{1}/4 mile you come to a lane; turn right. You are now back on the Dartmoor Way. After 300 metres turn left at the sign for Southlands Farm and follow the lane, track and lane back to North Bovey. Turn left at the village green and then left again for the car park.

8. Water to Drakeford Bridge

Start and finish: Although this stretch of the Dartmoor Way starts at Water, parking there is almost impossible. I therefore suggest starting at Pullabrook Wood, and that is where the route description begins. To reach the wood, take the road to Manaton from Bovey Tracey and turn right at Reddaford Water, following the sign for Lustleigh. Grid ref. 789801.

Parking: At the car park at Pullabrook Wood.

Length: 7.5km (4³/₄ miles)

Approximate time: 2¹/₂ hours

Degree of difficulty: B/C

Refreshments: A short detour in the middle of the walk, at Water, takes you to the Kestor Inn, a large pub with a comfortable bar, a light, airy dining room, a children's room and tables on the lawn outside. The food is home-made and ranges from delicious pasties and soups to a selection of pies and other main courses.

Route summary: The River Bovey and its tributary, the Becka Brook, are your companions for most of this walk, which is almost all through the lovely Bovey valley woods. It is a beautiful route at any time, but particularly so in spring, when the flowers and the fresh green leaves are an absolute delight. There is one very steep hill in the middle and a few muddy stretches, which together account for its B/C classification, but otherwise the going is quite easy.

Leave the car park and turn left to cross the River Bovey via Drakeford Bridge. At the junction on the other side turn left (signposted to Rudge). After 200 metres, as the lane climbs to the right, go through a gate on the left into

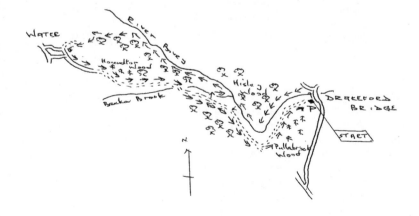

33

a field. Cross the field to a gate leading into Hisley Wood and follow the path on the other side. The hillside on the right is carpeted with bluebells in spring, and there is a wealth of other wild flowers all around you.

After about 800 metres/¹/₂ mile you will find Hisley Bridge, an old packhorse bridge, on your left. Cross it and go up across a muddy patch to a gate; turn right at the track on the other side (signposted to Manaton). Follow this track for about 350 metres until you come to a wooden bridge across the Becka Brook on the right, with a signpost pointing to the Bovey valley. Cross it and a stile on the other side, and follow the path to the right. After about 100 metres it swings sharp left and you join the River Bovey again. This next stretch is quite enchanting, especially in spring, with the river cascading over the rocks on your right and wild flowers galore all around you.

THE VIEW FROM HOUNDTOR WOOD

After about 1.5km/1 mile you come to a log bridge on the right; turn left (signposted to Manaton and Becky Falls). After 200 metres of steep climbing you come to a junction; go straight on (signposted to Water). You continue to climb, but slightly less steeply, and the path becomes rather wet but still quite passable. You go through a gate and follow the sunken path on the other side as it winds to the right and the left.

* At the top of the climb you come to a junction; go straight on (signposted to Manaton direct). Follow it round to the left, and at the next junction go straight on. At the next, go right for a short detour to the Kestor Inn if you are

in need of refreshment, or straight on to continue the walk (signposted to Lustleigh and the footpath to Trendlebere Down). After another 500 metres you pass a farm on your right and the lane becomes a track and swings right. Follow it to a gate into Houndtor Wood and then down to a junction. Turn left (signposted to Trendlebere Down). As you follow the track, you get some very good views across the valley through the trees on the right. The track leaves the wood and then enters it again, descending all the time. At the bottom the track swings right and crosses the Becka Brook via a bridge. It then swings left and follows the brook downstream.

After about 400 metres/¹/₄ mile you come to the junction where you turned off on the way out; go straight on (signposted to Trendlebere Down). At the next junction, at Hisley Bridge, do not turn left but go straight on again (signposted to the B3344 near Holne Brake). The track begins to climb, and after another 500 metres you will come to a big bank on the left; turn off here and go through the gate on the other side of the bank into Pullabrook Wood. Follow the track on the other side. After a short distance it forks; go right. At the next fork, follow the main track left down the hill. At the bottom you go through a gate into the car park. *

9. Drakeford Bridge to Bovey Tracey

Start and finish: Bovey Tracey. Grid ref. 814782.

Parking: The pay-and-display car park alongside the River Bovey in the centre of Bovey Tracey.

Length: 9km (5½ miles)

Approximate time: 3 hours

Degree of difficulty: B

Refreshments: There are several pubs and tearooms in Bovey Tracey. All have their attractions, but my favourite is the Old Thatched Inn, which is alongside the car park. It is a pretty, seventeenth-century coaching inn which comprises an old bar and a dining room, with a large chimney in between and stone fireplaces on both sides. The food is good pub grub and ranges from snacks to a good variety of main meals.

Route summary: The outward leg of this walk takes in part of the Templer Way, which follows the route down which granite from the Haytor quarries was taken to the docks in Teignmouth, before branching off to join the Dartmoor Way at Drakeford Bridge. It then follows the Way through pretty woodland back to Bovey Tracey. There is one steady climb near the start, but otherwise it is a very easy walk.

Turn left as you leave the car park. Just beyond the Brookside Café turn left down Newton Road. Take the second turning on the right, which is Avenue Road. At the T-junction at the end go straight on along a path. Go through a gate onto the main road and turn left and immediately right, following the public footpath sign. Go through a kissing-gate and follow a path alongside a stream. You pass a cross marking the grave of a Royalist officer killed during the English Civil War and come to a gate. Go through onto a track.

Follow the track, with a good view of Dartmoor ahead of you. It goes through a farmyard and turns left. Go through a gate and turn right just before a house, following the public footpath sign. After a few metres you will come to two gates; go through the right-hand one and follow the track on the other side. One more gate takes you onto a lane; turn right.

You are now on the Templer Way, which follows the route used to take granite from the Haytor quarries to the docks at Teignmouth in the nineteenth century. There it was shipped to London and other cities, where it was used in the construction of many public buildings. Along the left-hand side of the lane you can see the traces of the granite tramway that was built to transport the stone on the first leg of its journey to Teigngrace. There it was transferred to barges and taken down the Stover Canal and the River Teign to Teignmouth. It is a unique piece of industrial archaeology - the only tramway in the country made of granite. After about 300 metres the tramway swings left into a wood; carry on along the lane.

At the crossroads by the Edgemoor Hotel turn left, following the Templer Way waymark. The road climbs steadily, and after just over 1km/³/₄ mile you will find a track on the right, marked with the Templer Way waymark and a bridlepath sign pointing to the Bovey-Manaton road at Reddaford Water. Turn off here. You get a good view across the valley of the River Bovey as you follow the track and then a path through a belt of trees; on the other side the Templer Way goes left. You should go straight on, following the blue waymark. The path runs between fences and through a copse. It then widens to a track and emerges through a gate onto a road; cross over to a lane (signposted to Lustleigh). Follow the lane through a pretty wood and down a hill to the River Bovey at Drakeford Bridge.

* Cross the bridge and, at the junction on the other side, go straight on (signposted to Lustleigh and Moreton). Cross another small bridge and go under a railway bridge. At the next junction turn right (signposted to Bovey). Go under another bridge and soon you will meet the river again on your right. You go through another pretty wood, with a wealth of spring flowers alongside you. About 1km/¹/₂ mile after joining this lane you come to a T-junction; turn left, and at the next junction follow the main lane right up a hill. After a few metres turn right across a stile, following the public footpath sign, and after a few more metres go left up some steps.

The path takes you along the top of Parke Wood, with a disused railway line down on your right. Cross a stile into a field, which is full of violets and

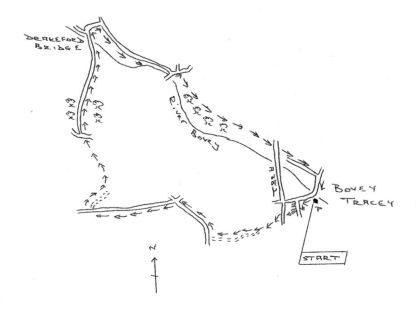

CROMWELL's ARCH,
BOVEY TRACEY

primroses in the spring. Go straight across to a kissing-gate back into the wood. You finally leave the wood via another kissing-gate. Follow a path on the other side between a hedge and a fence. You pass a pretty, thatched house and come out at a drive. Pass another thatched house and climb a short hill. At the top there is a junction; go right down an unsurfaced track. At the end turn left between a hedge and a wooden fence. Go through a kissing-gate and down to the main road.

Turn right and immediately left up some steps, following the public footpath sign to another kissing-gate. Follow a path to a playing field and keep to the left. At the end go left up some steps, following the yellow waymark. At the top you come to some houses; turn right. You pass a school on your left and a library on your right. You will see Cromwell's Arch on the left, part of the remains of a twelfth-century monastery. At the T-junction in the centre of the town turn right. You pass the Riverside Inn and the Devon Guild of Craftsmen's Riverside Centre. The latter is worth a visit for its displays of local crafts. Cross the river and the car park is on the left. *

10. Bovey Tracey to Sigford

A STABLE AT SIGFORD

Start and finish: Bovey Tracey. Grid ref. 814782.
Parking: The pay-and-display car park alongside the River Bovey in the centre of Bovey Tracey.
Length: 13km (8 miles)
Approximate time: 4¹/₂ hours
Degree of difficulty: C
Refreshments: See previous walk.
Route summary: Variety is the key to this exploration of a hidden corner of South Devon. There are farm fields, cool, green woods and some stunning viewpoints. The outward route follows the Dartmoor Way along flower-filled lanes, woodland tracks and open downland, while green lanes and more lanes bring you back to Bovey Tracey. There are a few steep climbs and one or two muddy stretches, but the views and the woodland flowers make the effort well worthwhile.

---

* Take the surfaced path that runs between the car park and the river. It soon leaves the river and follows a hedge. At the end it joins a road; follow that round to the right to a T-junction. Turn left and then, after a few metres, right down Ashburton Road (signposted to Brimley, the swimming pool and the Catholic church). You pass a church and then the swimming pool and a playing field. The road crosses a bridge over the main road, and about 100 metres further on there is a junction; bear right (signposted to Brimley and Ilsington). Take the second turning on the left, after about 400 metres/¼ mile, and at the crossroads after a few metres go straight on (signposted as unsuitable for long vehicles). This is a very pretty lane, fringed by hedges and a wealth of wild flowers and with good views on either side over the hedges. Follow it for about 2km/1¼ miles to Liverton.

The lane twists through the outskirts of the village to a T-junction. Turn right and, after 200 metres, left down a drive; there is a public footpath sign, but it is a few metres down the drive. This takes you to Woodgate Cottages and swings left to a wood. At the junction go straight on (signposted to

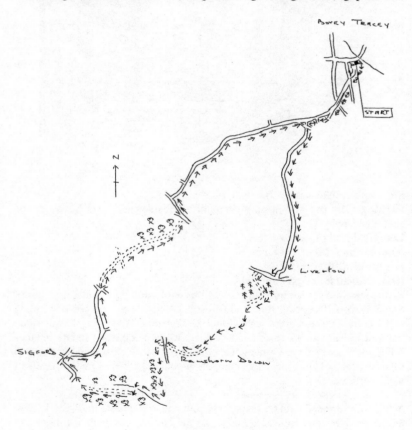

Ramshorn Down) and cross a stile to enter the wood. After a short distance you come to a cleared area; cross it to a track, following the path sign. Continue to climb, and at the next junction go straight on, following the path sign again. At the fork after a few metres go straight on again; this track takes you along the edge of the wood, still climbing. Then, when it swings to the right, go straight on up a path, following the sign.

Go through a gate and follow the path on the other side alongside a fence. At the end turn right just before a gate and follow a track. After 200 metres, as the fence swings left, go straight on. At the fork just beyond bear left and climb to a large open area fringed with gorse. Cross it and, as you do so, look right for an excellent view to Haytor. Go through a gap in the bank at the end and bear left, following the footpath sign. Go through a gate and bear left, still climbing. At the next fork bear right. This track takes you up to Ramshorn Down, where you are rewarded for the strenuous climb with the most spectacular panorama. To the left you can see almost to the sea and to the right you look out across Dartmoor, with Haytor on the horizon.

The track then begins to descend through the gorse and you come out at a lane. Cross to a track and follow it down to a concrete drive. Bear left and then right through a gate. Follow a rough path down a valley to a wood. At the T-junction go right (signposted to Bickington and Sigford) and cross a ladder stile and a footbridge. This stretch can become muddy after rain, but it is a very pretty wood, filled with bluebells in spring. Cross a stile and continue alongside the stream. Cross another stile and you come out into a field. Go straight across to a footbridge and a stile. Turn right on the other side and at the junction after a few metres go straight on (signposted to Sigford). This is another lovely bluebell wood. You are again following a stream; soon you go through a gate on the right and turn left to continue along the stream.

After another 200 metres the path turns left to cross a footbridge. Follow the track on the other side as it swings right. This is an easy track, but it can become muddy after rain. After a while you dip down to the right to a gate and continue along a path on the other side. You eventually leave the wood via another gate. Keep to the right of the field on the other side to yet another gate. Turn right in the lane on the other side and follow it to a T-junction. *

Turn right here, leaving the Dartmoor Way. At the first junction go straight on, but at the next turn right (signposted to Bickington). This lane climbs steeply for about 600 metres to a junction; go straight on. You now get a good view to your left. After another 700 metres you come to another junction; go straight on and bear left down a green lane. At the crossroads after 500 metres go straight on. The green lane now descends past a wood, which is carpeted with bluebells in spring, and ends at a road. Turn left and, after 400 metres/^{1}/4 mile, turn right up another lane. Cross a stream and climb the hill on the other side. At the junction go straight on (signposted to Brimley and Bovey Tracey). You now get a good view to the right.

This lane runs for about 1.5km/1 mile all the way back to Bovey Tracey. At the junction on the edge of town go straight on and you will find yourself on the road you took on the outward leg. When you reach the T-junction bear left, cross the main road and pass the playing field and swimming pool. At the end bear left again and, after a few metres, turn right down Indio Road. Take the path that bears right off the road to return to the car park.

11. Sigford to Ashburton

Start and finish: Ashburton. Grid ref. 755699.
Parking: In the pay-and-display car park off North Street and West Street.
Length: 11.5km (7 miles)
Approximate time: 4 hours
Degree of difficulty: B
Refreshments: There are a great many pubs, tearooms and restaurants to choose from in Ashburton. Café Green Ginger in East Street offers a good range of excellent food as well as teas and coffees, and has a lovely walled garden. The Studio, just opposite the car park, is a delightful old-world little tearoom, with low ceilings and good tea and coffee, although their menu is more restricted. If you are looking for a pub, try the Exeter Inn in West Street. It is a delightful twelfth-century hostelry with a cosy bar and lounge, and a lovely walled garden at the back. The food is not fancy, just good pub fare.
Route summary: This route mainly follows quiet, flower-filled lanes, but there are some lovely woodland stretches to provide variety, and some excellent views. Lanes and farm tracks take you north-east to Sigford, where you join the Dartmoor Way. Another lane and a green lane bring you back to the lovely Whiddon Scrubbs and a path which eventually emerges back in Ashburton. There is one steady climb in the middle, and a longer but more gentle one a little later, but the going is generally not too demanding.

Leave the car park via the North Street exit and turn right. At the T-junction turn left into East Street. Follow this road for about 800 metres/¹/₂ mile. Then, just before the derestriction sign, turn left along Balland Lane. Follow this lane past South Dartmoor Community College and you will come to Place Lane on the left. Just beyond it, as the lane swings right, go left and through a kissing-gate. There is a footpath sign pointing to the road near Waye Farm, but it is not easily visible from the lane. The path takes you past Place House and then swings left through a kissing-gate and right along a track. Go through a gate and follow the surfaced track on the other side. There is a lovely array of wild flowers in the hedgerows along here. You join another track; bear right. At the top, at Waye Court and Waye House, turn right again and you will soon reach a lane.

Turn left and follow the lane as it climbs. Like the track you have just left, it is fringed with wild flowers in season. It is a steady climb for almost 800 metres/¹/₂ mile, but at the top you are rewarded with a superb view ahead to the moor. Soon after reaching the top you come to a junction; go straight on. After another couple of hundred metres, just opposite the lane to Lower Whiddon Farm, there is a track on the right; take that. At the road at the end turn right. Follow this road for about 1.2km/³/₄ mile to a crossroads; turn left (signposted to Sigford). This lane runs alongside a pretty wood and then swings left into it, descending all the time. It then leaves the wood and you get a lovely view of a patchwork of fields across the valley of the River Lemon ahead. It continues to descend to the valley and then swings left.

 * You are now on the Dartmoor Way. Follow the lane alongside the pretty River Sig for another 250 metres to a T-junction. Turn left and follow this lane up into a delightful wood with yet another waterway, this time the Langworthy Brook, running alongside. The lane crosses the brook and wanders in and out of the trees, climbing gently as it does so. Alongside you can see spoil heaps from the tin and arsenic mines which operated here in the nineteenth and early twentieth centuries. After 1.5km/1 mile you come to a

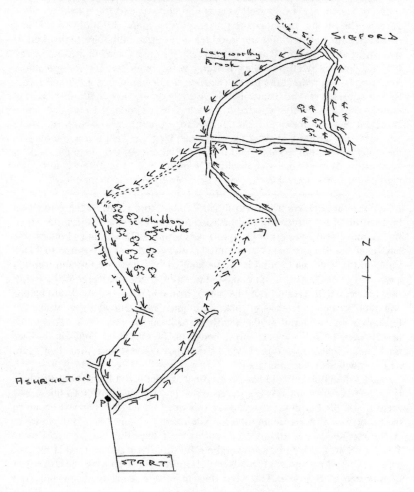

WATERLEAT
BRIDGE

crossroads; go straight across and, after 100 metres, turn right down a lane to Lower Whiddon Farm, which is signposted as a public footpath to Waterleat. You now get a very pleasant view ahead over fields and woods.

When the lane ends, go past a farmyard and swing left to join a green lane, which can become muddy at times. You still have the lovely view across the valley to the right, and to Boro Wood ahead. The green lane descends to the woodland of Whiddon Scrubbs and ends at a ford and a footbridge. Turn left onto a path (signposted to Ashburton). You now have a new river alongside you, the Ashburn. This is a particularly beautiful stretch, with the trees arching overhead and the water sparkling as it tumbles over the rocks on your right. After a while you will see a mill on the opposite bank, a sign of Ashburton's former position as a centre of the woollen industry.

You go through a kissing-gate and then, on the edge of the wood, you come to a junction; go straight on across a stile and continue along the side of the wood. At the end, cross a small rivulet and then a stile. A gate takes you into a field; keep to the right. You come out via a kissing-gate onto a lane; cross over to a stone stile. Keep to the right of the field beyond, alongside the river, to another stone stile. Keep to the right again, following the edge of the long field all the way round to the left and above some houses. At the end go through a kissing-gate and down some steps to a road; turn left and follow it back to the centre of Ashburton and the car park on the right. *

————————12. Ashburton to Buckfastleigh————————

Start and finish: Ashburton. Grid ref. 755699.
Parking: In the pay-and-display car park off North Street and West Street.
Length: 11.5km (7 miles)
Approximate time: 4 hours
Degree of difficulty: A/B
Refreshments: See previous walk for refreshments in Ashburton. If you want a break halfway through the walk, a short detour will take you to the Abbey Inn in Buckfast.
Route summary: Little-used lanes filled with colour are the main feature of this route, with a few green lanes, farm tracks and woodland paths to add variety. On the outward leg there is the opportunity, with a short detour, to visit the beautiful and interesting Buckfast Abbey. You also visit the ruins of Buckfastleigh's original church, alongside which is a tomb with both legendary and literary associations, and on your return to Ashburton you pass the historic St Lawrence Chapel. There are some excellent views, on both the outward and the return legs. Although there are one or two hills, only the climb up to the church at Buckfastleigh is unduly steep.

---

* Leave the car park into West Street and turn right. After 200 metres fork right up Bowden Hill. As the lane climbs, you get good views over to the left. When it ends, go straight on along a track. You soon join another track; go straight on again. You now get a superb view to your left over the A38 to the farmland beyond. After a while another stunning outlook opens up ahead over the Dart valley to the moor. You join a lane and descend past some houses to a junction; turn right (signposted to the Lavender House Hotel and Restaurant). Just beyond the hotel, turn sharp left down a track fringed with a superb array of wild flowers in season.

The track emerges at a road; go straight across. Follow a pretty lane for about 400 metres/¹/₄ mile past some houses. It then becomes a track and descends to a road. Turn right and follow the road for about 200 metres to the next junction; turn right up a lane. It climbs gently and at the top swings left. You get another good view ahead. When the lane swings right to a farm, go straight on along a path between hedges, following the public footpath sign. As you go, look to the right for another superb view over to the moor. This path can become overgrown and, although it is quite passable, shorts are not recommended. It comes out at a track and you will see the top of the tower of Buckfast Abbey on your right. The track comes out at the road again; turn right. After 800 metres/¹/₂ mile you come to a T-junction; turn right again.

You cross the River Dart and come to a roundabout. About 800 metres/¹/₂ mile along the road to the right is Buckfast Abbey. Established in the eleventh century and destroyed following the Dissolution of the Monasteries in 1539,

46

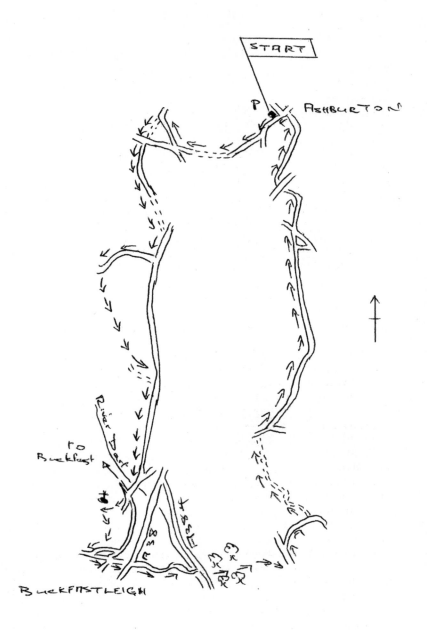

it was re-established in 1882. Under the leadership of Abbot Anscar Vonier, a new abbey church was built on the foundations of the original one, starting in 1906. It took five monks, only one of whom was trained as a stonemason, thirty-two years to complete. It is a lovely church, with a magnificent modern stained-glass window, and the whole complex is well worth a visit. About halfway to the abbey is the Abbey Inn if you feel in need of some refreshment.

To continue the walk, bear left at the roundabout and immediately right up Fairies Hall. This lane climbs for a short while and then ends; go straight on along a path, still climbing through a pretty wood, with a mass of wild garlic alongside in spring. When the path forks, go left and you will emerge at a turning circle, with the ruins of the church on your right. The church is 700 years old, but was destroyed in an arson attack in 1992. In the churchyard is the large tomb of Richard Cabell, a seventeenth-century squire who was believed to be so evil that he was buried under a stone slab; a special building was also constructed around the tomb to ensure that his ghost could not escape. It is said that, on dark and stormy nights, the ghosts of his hounds come howling round the tomb. The story served as the inspiration for Sir Arthur Conan Doyle's *The Hound of the Baskervilles*.

SQUIRE CABELL's TOMB, BUCKFASTLEIGH

The walk continues along a path on the left, opposite the church. It runs between hedges to a kissing-gate, beyond which are some stone steps. At the bottom you come out at a road; turn right and cross the River Mardle. At the T-junction at Fore Street turn left, leaving the Dartmoor Way. A short detour to the right takes you to the Valiant Soldier, a former pub which has been left exactly as it was when it closed in the 1950s. *

At the crossroads go straight across into Old Totnes Road (signposted to Beara, Colston, Luscombe and Velwell). Go under the A38 and follow the lane round to the left to cross a railway line. It then winds along to the River Dart and swings left to cross it. It joins a main road; turn right, proceeding with care as the road is busy. After 100 metres go left across a stile into a wood, following the public footpath sign. After a few hundred metres cross a footbridge and leave the wood via another stile. Keep to the left of the field on the other side, initially with the stream on your left. Climb gradually halfway up the hill on your left and you will come to a gate; turn right on the track on the other side and follow it to a lane.

Turn left and, after 150 metres or so, right along another lane, which winds down into a valley. After about 300 metres, just before you come to a house and the lane swings right, turn left along a green lane, following the public byway sign. This is a very attractive stretch as the flower-filled green lane meanders through the verdant farmland. After 800 metres/½ mile you pass a farm and emerge onto a lane; turn right. At the junction follow the main lane up to the left. It is delightful wandering along this quiet, pretty lane looking out over the fields and woods. The lane climbs gently and the view to the right improves as you ascend. Near the top you get a particularly good view between the hills to the farmland to the east, and at the top itself a magnificent view opens up ahead.

Some 1.6km/1 mile after joining the lane you come to a crossroads; go straight on (signposted to Ashburton). This lane descends and swings left under the A38. On the other side it swings right. You pass some industrial units and turn left past some houses into St Lawrence Lane. On the right is St Lawrence Chapel. Founded in the fourteenth century as a chantry chapel, it has served as a grammar school and as the meeting place of the ancient Court Leet and Court Baron. At the T-junction turn left into East Street and right into North Street. The car park is on the left.

13. Buckfastleigh to Holne

THE VALIANT SOLDIER,
BUCKFASTLEIGH

Start and finish: The Valiant Soldier, Fore Street, Buckfastleigh. Grid ref. 740661.

Parking: The closest car park to the start is at Station Road, but none is very far away, so park at whichever is most convenient.

Length: 11km (6¾ miles)

Approximate time: 3½ hours

Degree of difficulty: A/B

Refreshments: There are several pubs and cafés in Buckfastleigh. My favourite is the Singing Kettle, in Fore Street, just up the road from the start of the walk. It is an attractive old building with a large granite fireplace, which serves teas and coffees as well as a range of good-value meals, from soup or bread and cheese to mouth-watering main courses. If you want to break your journey halfway round, there is the Church House Inn at Holne.

Route summary: This varied route takes in three lovely woods interspersed with excellent views. Much of it follows little-used lanes fringed by hedges. It is a flower-lover's paradise, especially in spring, when both the woods and the hedgerows are filled with flowers. There is some climbing, especially in the middle, but only one stretch is particularly steep.

---

* Before you start, you might like to visit the Valiant Soldier. Once a pub, it is now a fascinating little museum, with the bar preserved as it was when it closed in the 1950s. Turn right outside and follow Fore Street to a fork at the

Globe Hotel. Go right into Chapel Street and follow that until it swings right into Market Street. When it does, go straight on into Jordan Street (signposted to Hapstead). At the junction on the edge of town go straight on along Jordan Street, which soon narrows to a lane as it leaves the town. You can hear the River Mardle down on your right as you follow this pretty lane. After about 600 metres you will see the entrance to Wotton Farm on your left, with a gate almost opposite it; there is a public footpath sign, but it is slightly hidden in the hedge. Turn off here, go round the gate and cross the narrow field on the other side. Go through another gate into a wood. Cross the river and swing left along a path fringed with bluebells and wild garlic in spring.

The path climbs away from the river, up the side of the valley, and after a while you will come to a fork; take the right-hand path, and fork right again after a few more metres. The path leaves the wood and emerges onto a lane; turn left. As you follow this lane you get a good view ahead of you to the moor. After 400 metres/¹/₄ mile you come to a T-junction; bear left. After another 200 metres you come to a crossroads; go straight on (signposted to Scorriton and Holne). Follow this lane for about 600 metres to a house called Burchetts Lodge. Turn right just before it up a track. Go through a gate marked with a blue waymark into Burchetts Wood.

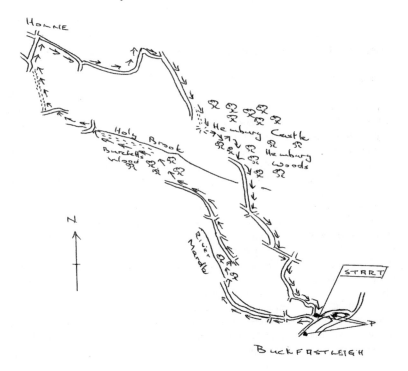

51

At the track junction go straight on. This wood is filled with bluebells in spring and with the sound of birdsong. At the next fork go straight on again, following the blue waymark. You descend to a track; turn left. You can now hear the Holy Brook on your right. Ignore the paths leading left up into the wood, just keep to the main track along the edge. Soon you will see the brook on your right. You pass the remains of a watermill's wheel pit on the left and then briefly join the brook. The track then swings away, only to rejoin it higher up. You then leave the wood and cross a footbridge to a lane; turn right.

Climb past some farm buildings and go through the second gate on the left. There is a public footpath sign, but it is not visible from this direction. Follow the clear path across a field, with more excellent views ahead of you. Ignore the paths that go right and left in the middle of the field, but carry straight on through some bracken and brambles to a stile. Continue along the path across the next field, and at the end follow the tree line up to the right to a stile leading onto another lane; turn left.

After 100 metres turn right up the drive for Langaford Cottage and then left through a gate. Cross a courtyard to a stile and keep to the left of a field to a gate leading into a green lane. Turn right and follow the green lane as it climbs steeply and then levels off. When it joins a lane, go straight on. At the next junction turn right into Holne. *

Just beyond the Church House Inn turn right to leave the Dartmoor Way (signposted to Buckfastleigh). As you follow this stretch of flower-filled lane, you get a good view to the right. After 600 metres, as the lane swings sharp right, go left (signposted to Shuttaford). You continue to enjoy excellent views to the right, but then the lane descends and swings left past a farm and then right across a stream. It climbs steadily out of the valley and at the top you come to a T-junction; turn right. You now get a superb view on the right to the moor, and soon another view opens up on the left.

After 700 metres you will come to a car park on the left; go through it to a gate into Hembury Woods. Take the right-hand track and keep going right, along the edge of the woods. They are a mass of wild flowers of different kinds in different seasons, including wood anemones, bluebells and self-heal, and also gorse and rowan. Go through a kissing-gate into Hembury Castle. This was the site of an Iron Age hill fort, and the wall and ditch can still be seen in places. You are free to wander at will and explore the area, but the path goes straight across the site. As you follow it, you will see a large mound on the right; this is all that remains of a small medieval motte and bailey castle. It probably had a wooden keep in the middle, with a wooden palisade around it.

The path crosses the defensive ditch and goes down to a stile. At the junction on the other side go straight on and, after a few metres, straight on again. At the third junction turn left, following the car park sign. This path winds down through the lovely wood. At the junction towards the bottom go straight on, following the car park sign again, and at the next junction turn right (again following the car park sign). You emerge at a lane; turn left and follow it as it winds steeply down through the woods. At the bottom it crosses the Holy Brook. At the T-junction go left and, after a few metres, as the lane swings left, go straight on (signposted to Buckfastleigh). Alternatively, you can turn left to visit Buckfast Abbey (see previous walk).

Climb briefly to a T-junction and turn left (signposted to Buckfast and Buckfastleigh). You now get a good view ahead of you. At the crossroads after 250 metres turn right (signposted to Buckfastleigh). The road swings left, then right, then left again past some industrial units. It then swings right again and ends at a T-junction with Chapel Street.

14. Holne to Dartmeet

Start and finish: Holne. Grid ref. 706694.

Parking: There is a public car park by the village hall, just down the road from the Church House Inn.

Length: 13km (8 miles)

Approximate time: 4¹/₂ hours

Degree of difficulty: C

Refreshments: The Church House Inn, in Holne, is hard to beat. It is a delightful fourteenth-century hostelry with dark beams, leaded windows and wooden partitions. There are several rooms, and tables on the grass outside, from which you can watch the world go by. The food is all home-made, from local ingredients where possible. If you want to break your walk halfway, try Badger's Holt restaurant and café at Dartmeet.

Route summary: The views on this walk are stunning, and the perspective changes regularly. It is mainly across moorland, but there are some beautiful wooded and riverside stretches as well. It is quite a challenging route, however, as there is rather a lot of climbing before you can enjoy the views. Moreover, at the start of the return leg there are also some stepping stones across the West Dart River, which become impassable after heavy rain. When this is the case, I am afraid there is no alternative but to either retrace your steps or make a detour of 1.5km/1mile.

---

* Turn right as you leave the car park and pass the Church House Inn. At the crossroads go straight on (signposted to Ashburton and Princetown). Climb out of the village and at the T-junction at the edge turn left (signposted to Hexworthy and Venford Reservoir). After a few metres go right across a stile, following the footpath sign to Newbridge. Follow the path on the other side between a hedge and a fence, with a good view ahead to the moor and Buckland Beacon on the horizon. Cross a stile into a field and cross to another stile. Go down the clear path diagonally right on the other side to a third stile and diagonally right again to a fourth. This leads you into Holne Woods.

Follow the path along the top of the woods, with the River Dart audible down below on the left. After a while it becomes visible and the path descends towards it. You come to a path junction; go straight on (signposted to Newbridge). You then meet up with the river and soon come to a fork; take the left-hand route, following the footpath sign. You leave the woods via a gate and a footbridge. Turn left at the road beyond and cross New Bridge.

Turn left on the other side (signposted to Hannaford) and pass a car park. Follow this road past a lovely lily pond and then up a hill. It passes a pretty rose-covered cottage and then winds past the entrance to Hannaford Manor, still climbing. You eventually emerge onto the open moor. After a bit more climbing the road levels off and you get a superb view ahead and to the right to Buckland Beacon. The road then joins a more major road. Bear left. (To avoid this short but fairly busy stretch of road, you can follow the path which runs alongside it on the left.)

After about 50 metres you will come to a clear track leading left, just by the Poundsgate village sign. Turn up here and then, after another 50 metres, go left onto a grassy track (the first one you come to). You now get a magnificent view over the Dart valley on the left. The track climbs gently and skirts round the hill on the right. As you come round the corner, you get a very good view ahead to Mel Tor, with Sharp Tor beyond it and Bench Tor across the valley. The track swings left alongside a wall and then right past Mel Tor. As it does so, another panorama opens up to the right, with a range of tors on the horizon.

Once past Mel Tor, the track winds right and then left between walls. When the right-hand wall goes to the right and the track peters out, go straight on alongside the left-hand wall. At the road at the end turn left and go down to cross a stream. Turn right immediately beyond to skirt round the foot of Sharp Tor. After 100 metres or so you will see a wall and fence among the gorse on your right; follow the line of that. Ahead of you now is Yar Tor.

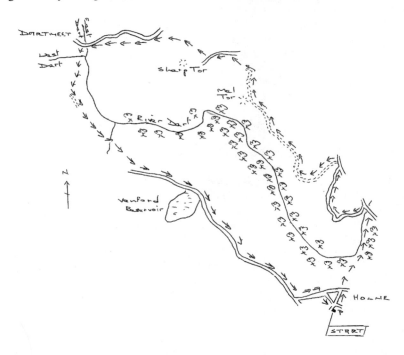

When the wall swings right, bear left across the head of a valley towards a car park. The banks you can see along here, one of which you cross, are the remains of prehistoric boundaries, called reaves. When you get to the car park turn left and follow the general line of the road down the hill. The road winds, but you can cut straight across. At the bottom, cross a cattle grid. Turn right for Badger's Holt or go straight on to continue the walk. Cross the bridge and on the other side bear left past a house and turn left, following the footpath and bridlepath signs. Go through a gate into a field. *

Turn left (signposted to Combestone via stepping stones). If the stones are impassable, you will either have to retrace your route or go right, up the field, to Huccaby, follow the road to Hexworthy and then on towards Holne to rejoin the main route further on - a detour of about 1.5km/1 mile. However, if all is well, go down to the river and cross via the stepping stones. Climb up away from the river on the other side, across an open stretch and through a wood. You go through a gateway into a field; keep left to a gap in a wall and keep left again. It is a steady climb out of the valley, but the views as you go are superb.

Halfway up this field you will find a sign pointing left to the Holne road near Venford Reservoir. Turn off and follow a surfaced track. At the end bear right, following the bridlepath sign, and go through a gate. The track is initially bounded by walls, but these turn away to form a narrow field. Go through a small wooded area and then another small field to a gate. Beyond that you are back on open moorland. When the wall alongside you swings right, go straight on along the path. It takes you down to a stream and swings left to cross it. Bear right on the other side to join a slightly sunken path, which crosses two leats as it climbs.

It comes out onto a road; turn left and follow the line of the road to a car park. Cross the wall of Venford Reservoir on the other side. The banks can be very pretty, especially when the rhododendrons are out. When you leave the reservoir, follow the line of the road up a small hill. As you come over the brow, another stunning panorama opens up ahead of you. About 1.5km/1 mile after crossing the reservoir you cross a cattle grid. Another 500 metres further on there is a junction; follow the main lane round to the left (signposted to Holne). Another 500 metres further on is another junction; turn right (signposted to Holne village centre and Buckfastleigh). The lane winds down to the Church House Inn; turn right to return to the car park.

15. Dartmeet to Swincombe

Start and finish: Dartmeet. Grid ref. 672733.
Parking: In the car park at Dartmeet.
Length: 10km (6¼ miles)
Approximate time: 3½ hours
Degree of difficulty: B/C
Refreshments: Badger's Holt, just beyond the car park at Dartmeet, is a very pleasant restaurant, café and gift shop, with a large, spacious dining area inside and tables out on the grass alongside the river. A wide range of food is available, from sandwiches and soup to pies and restaurant meals. There is also the Forest Inn at Hexworthy, which entails a short detour about 2km/1¼ miles into the walk (you also pass close to it on the return leg). It is a fairly modern pub, friendly and welcoming and with a good range of food on offer.
Route summary: Most of this walk is across open moorland, with the rolling hills stretching away in all directions and a range of tors dominating the horizon. There are also one or two lovely woodland and riverside stretches, however, to add variety. The outward leg follows the Dartmoor Way to the abandoned farmstead of Swincombe, and you return via moorland and field paths and a quiet, gorse-fringed road. There are several hills, although most are fairly short. There are also some stepping stones to negotiate at the end, which become impassable after heavy rain. There is an alternative return route which avoids the stones, but it is not as interesting.

* Leave the car park via the vehicle entrance and turn right to cross the East Dart River. On the other side bear left past a house and turn left beyond it, following the footpath sign. Go through a gate and bear right on the other side, following the footpath sign for Huccaby. Follow the waymarked posts up the field. Towards the top the path swings to the left and you get a good view left across the river. Go through a gateway and turn right up a rocky track between walls, still climbing. Cross a stile and continue along the track on the other side. Go through a gate towards the top and turn left. Follow the path through the gorse and at the top you get some magnificent views, both ahead and behind you.

Follow the waymarked posts across the field to a gate and go down the track on the other side. At the T-junction after a few metres turn right, and at the lane a few metres further on turn left. You pass a church and can see the West Dart River on your right. You cross Hexworthy Bridge and on the other side you will see a stone stile on your right; cross it and turn left to follow a path up a field. At the end, cross another stone stile and follow the path in the next field to the far right-hand corner. Go through a gap in the wall on the right and then turn immediately left across a stone stile, following the path sign.

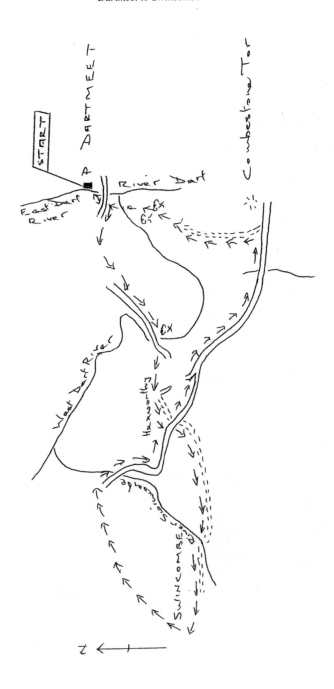

Go through a gate at the end and then another two as you cross a farmyard. After the last one turn right and follow a concrete track up a short hill. (If you want to visit the Forest Inn, turn left and follow a lane for about 200 metres.) When the concrete track ends, continue along the rough track ahead. This joins a surfaced track; turn left and after a few metres you will come to a road. Cross it to a rough track and go through a gate. You now have a stunning panorama through almost 360 degrees. When the wall on your right goes right, follow it round. The track goes through a gap in a wall and a gate, and continues on the other side. The wall falls away to the right, but you should continue along the clear track that goes straight on. It becomes slightly less clear further on, but you have the wall down on your right to give you your direction.

Soon you will see the River Swincombe ahead of you, with a clear track coming in from the left and a footbridge across the river. Aim for the bridge and cross it. Bear left on the other side, alongside a tumbledown wall, following the wet and stony track. It takes you among the ruins of Swincombe. At the path junction go straight on between two walls. At the end of the walls go straight on along a clear path to a gate leading onto the open moor. Follow the path on the other side alongside a wall on the right. After about 400 metres/¼ mile you will come to a junction. Turn right and go through a gate, following the signpost for Sherberton. *

A RUINED FARMSTEAD,
SWINCOMBE

Follow the grassy track on the other side and, as you come over the brow of the hill, you will have a superb view across the northern moor, with a range of tors on the horizon, from Longaford Tor and Higher White Tor on the left, through Bellever Tor and Laughter Tor in the middle, to Yar Tor and Sharp Tor on the right. In the middle of this field you will come to a path junction marked with a post; go straight on, following the arrow pointing to Sherberton. At the end go through a gate and bear right. The path becomes less clear, but if you keep to the line of the wall on the right you will be all right. You will meet a track coming in from the left; bear right to a gate and follow the track on the other side down to a farmyard. Bear right in the yard and go through it to a gate leading onto a road.

The road takes you down to cross the River Swincombe and swings right and then left. As you climb out of the valley you can see the remains of the Gobbett Tin Mine on your right, and then a long gully. This is called a girt, and was formed by miners digging into the hillside in search of the precious ore. You go over a cattle grid and, after another 200 metres or so, cross your outward route. If there has been a lot of rain, or you are concerned about the stepping stones, turn left here along the surfaced track and retrace your route back to Dartmeet via Hexworthy Bridge and Huccaby.

Otherwise, continue along the road for another 500 metres to a T-junction; turn right (signposted to Holne) - or left for a short detour to the Forest Inn. The road winds down for about 1.2km/^{3}/4 mile to the interestingly named O Brook. It crosses the brook and climbs up the opposite side. It is a steep climb, but the view from the top makes it worthwhile. At the top, just before you come to Combestone Tor, you will find a track on the left. Take it, and follow it round the hill and across a leat to a gate. At the junction just beyond go straight on along the main track. Cross a cattle grid and, when the track swings right through a wall to a house, go straight on alongside the wall, following the sign for Dartmeet. Go through a gap in a wall and keep right in the next field. Go through another gap and into a wooded area. At the bottom are the stepping stones across the West Dart River. Cross over and go up a field to a gate; turn right past the house and right at the road beyond. Cross the East Dart and the car park is on the left.

16. Swincombe to Princetown

Start and finish: Princetown. Grid ref. 589735.
Parking: There is a public car park behind the High Moorland Visitor Centre in the centre of Princetown.
Length: 11km (6³/₄ miles)
Approximate time: 3¹/₂ hours
Degree of difficulty: A
Refreshments: There are three pubs, a tearoom and two cafés in Princetown. My favourite is the Plume of Feathers. With its granite walls, stone floor, copper bar and open fires, it is full of atmosphere, while outside there are a beer garden and children's play area. The menu is wide-ranging, and the food freshly cooked.

Route summary: This route takes you across typical moorland - rolling, grassy uplands where the views, the sense of space and the wide skies will captivate you. The outward leg takes you in a wide sweep to the south, through industrial remains and past a notorious bog, before heading north to join the Dartmoor Way just above the River Swincombe. You return to Princetown along the Way, which here follows a track with an interesting history. Although it is quite a long route the terrain is very easy, hence its A classification. There is one short stretch where navigation could be tricky in very poor visibility, but since the main feature of the walk is the views, it is unlikely that you will be attempting it in such conditions.

Leave the car park and turn right past the High Moorland Visitor Centre. At the crossroads go straight across, passing between the Plume of Feathers and the Railway Inn. Go through a gate and follow the track on the other side between walls to the moor. Look back as you go for a good view of the grim Dartmoor Prison which dominates Princetown. Go through another gate and continue along the track, now with the wall only on the left. Ahead of you, you will see South Hessary Tor, with Hart Tor to your right.

Stop at South Hessary Tor for a superb view to both left and right, which gives you a good idea of the vastness of the moor. Continue to follow the track, and after about 1.5km/1 mile you will cross a track. Another lovely view opens up to the right, with Burrator Reservoir and Sheep's Tor in the middle distance. After another 400 metres/¹/₄ mile you will come to another track. Turn left here and follow the track down to a road, crossing another track on the way. Go straight on along the road. You cross the Devonport Leat, which was constructed in the eighteenth century to supply water to Devonport, now part of Plymouth. It ran for some 43km/27 miles across the inhospitable moor and, as you can see, is still in working order, although it now empties into Burrator Reservoir. The road ends at the remains of the Whiteworks Tin Mine. To your right are the notorious Foxtor Mires, the

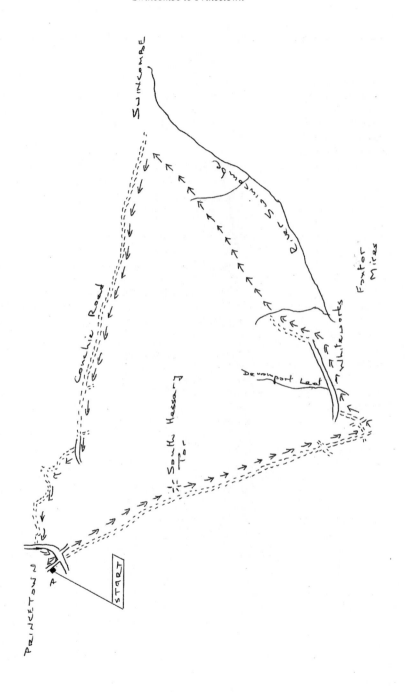

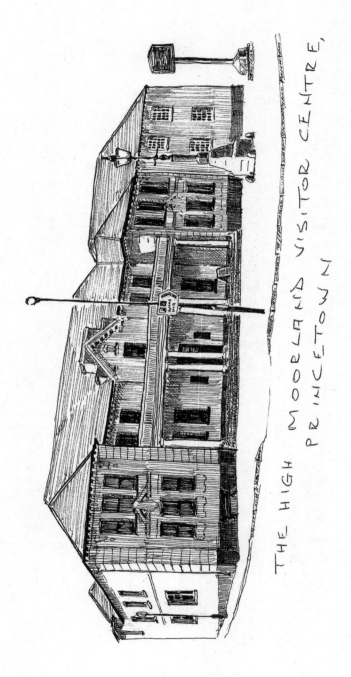

THE HIGH MOORLAND VISITOR CENTRE, PRINCETOWN

inspiration for the Great Grimpen Mire in Sir Arthur Conan Doyle's great Sherlock Holmes mystery, *The Hound of the Baskervilles*.

At the end of the road go straight on along a track to a gate. Beyond the gate the track curves right and then left to a stream. Cross the stream and follow the path up the hill on the other side. As you go, you get another good view of the moor to your right. Go over the hill to another stream. The path peters out after a while, but you should be able to find your way over the moor without difficulty. Carry straight on, with the valley of the River Swincombe a few hundred metres over on your right, aiming for Bellever Tor and Bellever Forest behind it, which you will see on the horizon. It is not necessary to be precise, because you can always correct for any error when you come over the rise.

* About 2.5km/1½ miles after leaving Whiteworks you will come to a path; turn left along it and you will soon find a fence on your right. You are now on the Dartmoor Way. This track is known as the Conchie Road because it was built by conscientious objectors ('conchies') who were detained in Dartmoor Prison during the First World War. It stretches from Princetown to just about where you joined it, where it comes to an abrupt stop - leading one to assume that it was not intended to lead anywhere, just to give the detainees some hard labour in case they found their time in prison too easy!

Follow the Conchie Road for 2.5km/1½ miles, ignoring two tracks leading left along the way, to a gate. As you go, you get another superb view to the right, with a range of tors on the horizon, including Higher White Tor, Longaford Tor and Beardown Tors. Follow the lane on the other side of the gate and, just beyond the house on the right, turn right (signposted 'path'). Go through another gate and follow a track which bends left and then right. At the junction turn left (signposted to Princetown) and cross the Devonport Leat again. Go through another two gates, with a final superb view to your right, and follow a track as it winds between walls to a road. Turn left to return to Princetown and soon you will find the Visitor Centre on your right and the Plume of Feathers on your left. *

17. Princetown to Ingra Tor

Start and finish: Princetown. Grid ref. 589735.
Parking: There is a public car park behind the High Moorland Visitor Centre in the centre of Princetown.
Length: 11.5km (7¼ miles)
Approximate time: 3½ hours
Degree of difficulty: A
Refreshments: See previous walk.
Route summary: You are never without a stunning view on this superb walk - and you can enjoy them without much climbing! It is virtually all open moorland, with the hills rolling away into the distance in every direction and a constant succession of tors dominating the horizon. A long way from traffic and towns, it is beautifully peaceful, with only the songs of the skylarks to break the silence. This leg of the Dartmoor Way follows the track of a disused railway with an interesting history, past some industrial remains. You return across a stretch of farmland and then more open moorland. There is one short climb in the middle, and a short stretch when you have to pick your way across open grassland without a clear path, but otherwise the route is all level and easy.

---

* Leave the car park via the vehicle exit and turn left. Pass the fire station and turn left onto a path just beyond it, following the sign for the disused railway. It swings right and goes through a gate onto open moorland to join a track. This is the route of the Plymouth and Dartmoor Railway. It was the brainchild of Sir Thomas Tyrwhitt, a local landowner and the founder of Princetown, who wanted to open up this part of the moor and 'civilise' it by encouraging cultivation and exploiting the granite reserves. The intention was that it would bring in lime and sea sand to make the land more fertile so that crops could be grown, and carry granite, peat and produce down to Plymouth. Opened in 1823, it was originally a horse-drawn tramway, but the plan to open up the moor for cultivation failed, and virtually the only income came from the transport of granite from the quarries. It was changed to take steam trains in 1883, but closed in 1956.

As you follow this stretch, you get the first of a succession of views. Ingra Tor is visible ahead of you, with Leeden Tor and Sharpitor over to the left. About 1.5km/1 mile after you joined it, the track swings to the right and you come to a junction. Go straight on and, where the track forks, take the left-hand route. You can now see across to the northern moor, with Great Mis Tor half right and Great Staple Tor and Middle Staple Tor half left. On your right are the spoil heaps of Foggintor Quarries, the first of the granite workings you will come across in this area, and ahead of you, below Great Staple Tor, Merrivale Quarry, the last granite quarry on Dartmoor to close, in 1997. This

area was famous for its granite, which was shipped all over the country in Victorian times and used in the building of many of our most famous buildings, including the British Museum and Nelson's Column.

The track then swings left around King's Tor and passes through a cutting, with more signs of quarrying activity. As you emerge from the cutting, another lovely view comes into sight to the right, across the green West Devon countryside to Cornwall, a contrast to the barren moorland that has surrounded you so far. When the track forks, the Dartmoor Way follows the right-hand, lower route. However, you might like to follow the higher track for a couple of hundred metres to see a strange phenomenon - beautifully carved corbels lying alongside the track. These were cut for the widening of London Bridge in 1903, but were not needed - and there they have lain ever since.

CORBELS INTENDED FOR LONDON BRIDGE, SWELLTOR QUARRIES

Back on the lower track you will pass Swelltor Quarries on your left, and then the track swings right. It crosses a stream and then goes under a bridge. You pass Ingra Tor, with more signs of quarrying, on the left and then cross a wooden bridge. Shortly afterwards, as the railway swings left around the tor, branch off right and make your way down the hill. There are various paths and it does not matter too much which you take, as they all lead down to a track. *

When you reach the track, turn right and follow it back to a cattle grid. Continue on the other side. Just after the track swings left to a house turn right onto a rocky path, following the public bridlepath sign. Follow the succession of waymarked posts which winds up a field. At the top go through a gate back onto the disused railway. Cross it and make your way across the moorland to the right of Swelltor Quarries. A short detour to the left will enable you to explore the main quarry itself. Otherwise, aim for the far corner of the wall you will see on your right, where there is a track. When you get there, follow the track round to the right and then to the left. You come out at a junction in the dismantled railway; cross over and bear right. Do not take the main track, which bears left. There is no path, but if you aim to the right of the mast at the top you will be heading in the right general direction. As you come over the brow of the hill, you will see the square bulk of South Hessary Tor on the horizon half right and soon the dismantled railway will come into view below you, on the right. You now have a choice: you can either go down to join it and follow it as it winds back to Princetown, or you can keep above it and cut straight across the moor. The railway track provides easier walking conditions but is a little further, while going above it is more direct but not quite as easy. If you go across the moor, you will rejoin the track just before the small plantation on the edge of Princetown. Follow the path at the end and pass the fire station to return to the car park.

18. Ingra Tor to Warren's Cross

Start and finish: Merrivale. Grid ref. 539750.
Parking: In the car park just to the west of Merrivale on the B3357.
Length: 12km (7¹/₂ miles)
Approximate time: 4 hours
Degree of difficulty: B
Refreshments: The Dartmoor Inn at Merrivale, which you pass after about 1km/¹/₂ mile, is a delightful seventeenth-century pub comprising a long lounge bar with a large granite fireplace and a smaller public bar. There are also tables out on the grass in front, overlooking the valley of the River Walkham. There is a good selection of main courses on offer as well as bar snacks such as ploughman's lunches, soups and salads.
Route summary: This is a very varied walk, ranging from shady woods to open moors and farmland. One thing that is almost constant, however, is the views. Wherever you are on the route, they are never less than stunning. From Merrivale, tracks and paths take you south through woodland above the River Walkham to join the Dartmoor Way just west of Ingra Tor. This leg of the Way follows quiet lanes and roads through the pretty hamlet of Sampford Spiney and out onto the open moor. At Warren's Cross you leave it and head north along another little-used lane. A green lane takes you back onto the open moor for the final leg back to the car park.

Turn left as you leave the car park and follow the road down towards Merrivale. The views start immediately: moorland stretching out to the horizon all around, with Great Mis Tor half left, Ingra Tor half right and Vixen Tor immediately on the right. As you descend to Merrivale, you will find a leat on your right and then you pass the Dartmoor Inn and cross the River Walkham. Start climbing the hill on the other side, but when you come to a farm after 150 metres or so turn right, following the bridlepath sign. Pass to the right of a house and go through a gate. Follow the track on the other side, enjoying the view down the wooded valley of the Walkham as you go.

The track becomes surfaced and you go through a gate into a farmyard. Go through another gate and follow the grassy track on the other side round to the left to yet another gate. The path on the other side takes you down into a wood to cross a stream. It is lovely here, as the path meanders among moss-covered rocks and stunted trees, with bluebells covering the ground in spring. Go through another gate and follow the path among a mixture of trees and gorse on the other side, with another wonderful view on the right. You then find yourself between ancient walls and go through two gates to a track between high stone walls. Another two gates in quick succession take you onto open ground. Cross it to a lane and a gate, and follow the lane as it winds down between high banks for just over 1km/³/₄ mile to a crossroads.

* This is where the Dartmoor Way comes down from Ingra Tor. Turn right (signposted to Ward Bridge and Woodtown) and follow this new lane down into a wood to cross the River Walkham again. It climbs steeply up the other side before levelling off. Cross a cattle grid and, immediately after it, turn right up a track (signposted as unsuitable for motors). After 400 metres/¹/₄ mile it joins a lane; go straight on. After 200 metres you come to a junction; fork left. The lane winds past the hamlet of Sampford Spiney, with a field of alpacas on the left and the church on the right. It comes out at a T-junction, with open moorland ahead.

Turn left and follow the line of the road, with the best view yet ahead of you - on a clear day you can see Bodmin Moor in the distance. At the junction, after 700 metres, go straight on (signposted to Whitchurch Down). At the next junction bear right (signposted to Whitchurch Down again). If you look half right now, you can see the unmistakable shape of Brent Tor on the horizon, with its church perched on top, and to the right are Cox Tor and Great Mis Tor. Another 700 metres further on, there is another junction; turn right (signposted to Princetown). *

After 300 metres you will come to another junction; go straight on (signposted to Tavistock and Princetown). At the next junction go straight on again (signposted to Tavistock and Princetown again). You go down to a cattle grid and then climb a hill on the other side for 500 metres to the main road. Go straight across (signposted to Peter Tavy). After 600 metres turn

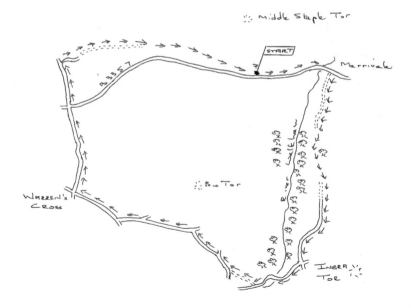

A WAYSIDE CROSS,
SAMPFORD SPINEY

right (signposted to Collaton). Follow this lane as it winds and climbs past some houses and a farm. When it ends, go left round some farm buildings to a green lane.

Climb steadily up the green lane and, after 500 metres, go through a gateway onto a much broader track. You now have Cox Tor half left and, if you look back, you get another superb view to Bodmin Moor. A gate leads you onto the open moor; follow the track straight ahead as it crosses a road and climbs gently. As you come over the brow of the hill, you will see the road to your right. Follow the track for about 600 metres until it starts to curve to the left. Branch off then and take one of the many narrow paths which run down towards the road. Follow the line of the road for about 800 metres/$^1/_2$ mile to the car park.

——19. Warren's Cross to Peter Tavy Cross ——

Start and finish: Tavistock. Grid ref. 480741.

Parking: The Riverside long-stay car park. Follow the signs for long-stay parking.

Length: 11.5km (7 miles)

Approximate time: 4 hours

Degree of difficulty: C

Refreshments: As one would expect in a town its size, there are a number of places to obtain refreshments in Tavistock - pubs, restaurants and cafés. I particularly like the East Gate Café and Brasserie in Market Road. It is a well-furnished and decorated establishment in an attractive old building, but its main attraction is the riverside terrace outside. It serves a wide range of meals and snacks as well as hot and cold drinks all day, but not in the evening.

Route summary: This leg of the Dartmoor Way runs from Warren's Cross on Whitchurch Down through the attractive market town of Tavistock to Peter Tavy Cross. For convenience, however, our route takes it in two 'bites'. The first follows the second section out of Tavistock and along little-used lanes up the hillside above the River Tavy to Peter Tavy Cross. More quiet lanes bring you south again to Warren's Cross, where you start the first section. This crosses Whitchurch Down and returns you to Tavistock. Alternatively, if you would prefer to do the whole leg as one stretch, there is parking not far from Warren's Cross and you can start there.

The views on this stretch are outstanding and it is almost all along lanes, so there is no mud or rough ground to contend with. However, the views come at a price: there are a number of steep hills to negotiate before you can enjoy them.

Go to the end of the car park and take the surfaced path that runs above the River Tavy. At the end you join a road by a roundabout. Cross to Dolvin Road, which is signposted to Okehampton. If you are so inclined, you can take a short detour to the left across the river to explore the centre of this attractive town, including historic Bedford Square and the ancient Court Gate, one of the few remnants of Tavistock Abbey.

* Follow Dolvin Road to another roundabout and fork right into Mount Tavy Road, still following the sign for Okehampton. After about 200 metres there is a junction; turn right, still following Mount Tavy Road (signposted to Princetown). Then, after a few metres, turn right again up Green Hill. Climb this steep hill to a T-junction; turn left here into Violet Lane (signposted to Princetown). As you go down this road, you get a good view of the imposing buildings of Mount House School ahead and Kelly College on the left. At the T-junction at the bottom turn right (signposted to Princetown again). There is

COURT GATE, TAVISTOCK

a path alongside the road. When it ends, continue along the road for a short distance to a junction; turn left into a lane, following the waymark for the West Devon Way.

This lane climbs past the rear entrance to Mount House School and then the entrance to Tavistock Trout Fishery. It then deteriorates into a track and continues to climb. As it does so, you get an excellent view to the left over the hedge. Brent Tor, with its Church of St Michael perched precariously on top, is clearly visible. It then levels off for a while and becomes a surfaced lane once more. It swings right and, after 300 metres, left again and begins to climb. At the top you get another excellent view across to the moor, with Cox Tor straight ahead. It swings left again, descends steeply and swings right, emerging eventually at a crossroads. This is where you temporarily leave the Dartmoor Way. *

Turn right (signposted to Princetown and Horrabridge). You are now faced with another climb. At the junction at the top of the hill go straight on (signposted to Princetown). Through the gateways on the left you can now see Cox Tor again. At the next junction go straight on again, and again at the next. Another 600 metres brings you out at a main road; go straight across (signposted to Whitchurch Down and Moortown). The lane descends to cross a stream and then a cattle grid, and then climbs up the hill on the other side. You can console yourself, however, that this is the last climb on this route. At the next two junctions go straight on (signposted to Whitchurch Down and

Sampford Spiney). You now get a very good view of the moor to your left, with Pew Tor in the middle distance and Ingra Tor further away.

* At the top you come to the junction at Warren's Cross, which is where you rejoin the Dartmoor Way. Turn right (signposted to Whitchurch Down) and follow the line of the road. It is not necessary to stick religiously to the road itself; as long as you follow its direction, you can take advantage of the short grass between the bracken and gorse alongside. A superb view opens up ahead of you - on a clear day you can see all the way to Bodmin Moor - and to the right. As you cross the down, you will soon find a golf course on your right.

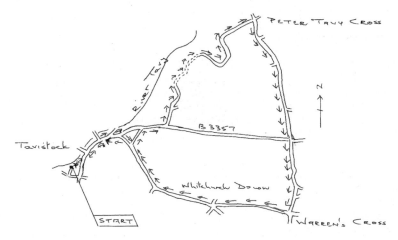

A little over 1km/³/₄ mile after joining the Dartmoor Way you come to a five-way junction. Follow the main road half right (signposted to Tavistock). At the end of the golf course, when it swings left, go straight on and cross a cattle grid. Follow the road down on the other side through the outskirts of Tavistock. When it turns right into Violet Lane, go straight on. After about 150 metres you will see a public footpath sign on the left; go through a kissing-gate. Do not follow the clear path across the field on the other side but bear right to descend gently. You enter a belt of trees and then you will find a stile on your right. Cross it and go down some steps on the other side to a road; turn left. You are now back on your outward route. At the roundabout bear left (signposted to Plymouth and the town centre). At the next roundabout cross over into Whitchurch Road and follow the path on the right, back to the car park. *

—— 20. Peter Tavy Cross to North Brentor ——

Start and finish: Peter Tavy. Grid ref. 513777.
Parking: In the road in Peter Tavy; please park with consideration for others.
Length: 13km (8 miles)
Approximate time: 4 hours
Degree of difficulty: B
Refreshments: The Peter Tavy Inn is a delightful fifteenth-century pub. It has three rooms, all with slate floors and low beams, and two with wood-burning stoves. There are also tables outside. The food ranges from baguettes and jacket potatoes to a variety of award-winning main courses.
Route summary: This leg of the Dartmoor Way takes you to Peter Tavy's better-known 'twin' village of Mary Tavy and then along the flank of Gibbet Hill, with a superb panorama all around. Having skirted the village of North Brentor, we leave the Way and climb Gibbet Hill, enjoying more outstanding views at the top. The route then descends to the outskirts of Mary Tavy and follows paths and tracks across the Tavy valley back to Peter Tavy. It is a relatively easy route apart from one steady climb across open moorland, with no clear path, in the middle.

Head south along the main lane through Peter Tavy (to the right if you are starting from the church or the Peter Tavy Inn). Follow it out of the village and after about 800 metres/¹/₂ mile you will come to a junction; turn left. At the next junction go straight on. The lane swings right and you come out at Peter Tavy Cross. Turn right (signposted to Tavistock).

* You are now on the Dartmoor Way. You get a good view ahead and to the right across the moor. Follow the lane down a hill to a T-junction; turn left (signposted to Tavistock) and cross the River Tavy. Immediately on the other side turn right up the drive for Beggars Hatch, following the public footpath sign. At the end go through a gate and bear right across the field on the other side to a gateway in a rather tumble-down wall. Cross the next field to a stile, with an excellent view to the right to White Tor. Cross another field to a gap in a wall and follow the path on the other side alongside a belt of gorse on the right. As you cross the field, you will meet a hedge on the right; follow it to a gate. Keep to the left of the next field, passing a granite gateway without a fence alongside it. You now have Peter Tavy across the valley on your right.

Cross a stile at the end, but don't cross the next field; instead go through the gate on the right and turn left, keeping to the left of another field. You now have the river immediately below you on the right. Go through a gateway at the end, and at the path junction halfway along the next field go straight on to a gate. Keep to the left again, still with a good view of the moor on the right. The path descends to a belt of trees and you will find a stile on the left.

Cross it and bear right down a green lane. At the end cross a footbridge across the Cholwell Brook on the right and climb to a lane.

Turn left into Mary Tavy. You pass the church and come to a T-junction; turn right (signposted to Horndon). Pass a school, and at the next junction go

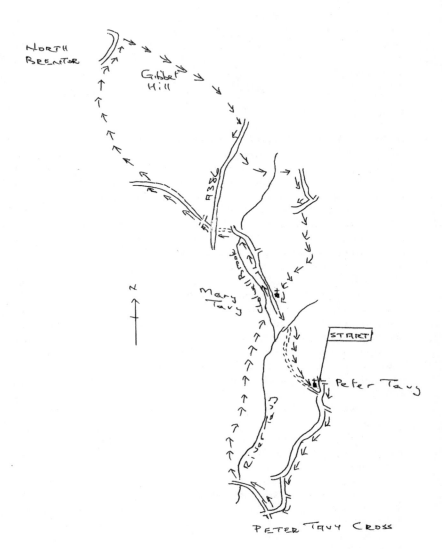

BRENT TOR

straight on. Cross the Cholwell Brook again and then, as the lane swings right, go left up a track, following the public bridleway sign. You come out at a main road; cross over to Brentor Road. At the crossroads go straight on. You eventually cross a cattle grid leading onto the open moor. You now get a lovely view ahead with Brent Tor and its church on the horizon.

After a few metres turn right onto a stony track and immediately left onto a broad grassy path, following the West Devon Way waymark. Look back for a wonderful view across western Dartmoor. You pass a cairn and another magnificent panorama opens up ahead of you, still with Brent Tor on your left. The path curves to the right round Gibbet Hill and you will see the tower of North Brentor church half left. As you skirt the village, you will see a road on your left and the path descends gently to join it. *

When the road goes sharp left, turn right, following the blue bridleway waymark to leave the Dartmoor Way. The path climbs steadily up Gibbet Hill until it crosses a grassy track. On the other side the path is less clear. When you come to another grassy track, bear left and then go right to continue climbing the hill. When the track contours round to the left, bear right off it, still climbing. There is no clear path here, but the going is relatively easy, and as long as you are climbing rather than contouring you will be all right - you can always correct for any slight deviation from the direct route when you get to the top.

You will soon see a mound on the summit of Gibbet Hill; aim to the right of that. As you come over the hill another stunning view of the moor appears ahead of you. You will pass two disused mineshafts which have been fenced off and then you will see the main road below you, with the Mary Tavy village sign to the right. Go down towards it and you will come to a track; bear right along that. At the bottom you will find a gate with a kissing-gate alongside; go through and onto the road. Turn right and follow the road.

After 200 metres go left down a track; there is a footpath sign, but it is some distance from the road. Go through a gate and follow the track on the other side. It winds down to a farmyard; cross to a gate on the left and go through another gate. Bear right to descend to the Cholwell Brook, where you will find a footbridge and a stile. Cross both and make your way through the trees on the other side, bearing slightly right to cross a stile. Bear left across a rather boggy stretch to a stone stile into a lane. Turn right, and at the T-junction after 400 metres/¹/₄ mile right again. After another 100 metres turn left across a stile and bear right across the field beyond to a ladder stile in the far corner.

Make your way through the gorse and bracken on the other side, keeping to the left. Cross a track, go through a gap in a wall and keep to the left again. At the end of this field you come to another track; go left through a gate and then through another one. At the end of the next field go right through a gate and follow a track to the left of a wall and past a ruined chimney to a stile. Keep to the right of the next field and at the end go left and follow the boundary to a gate on the right. Go through and keep to the right to a stone stile leading into Mary Tavy churchyard. Go round to the left and then right around the church, and you will come out at a lane.

You are now back on the Dartmoor Way. Follow it for a short distance, but at the end of the lane, when the Way goes right, go straight on (signposted to Peter Tavy). Follow a green lane down and go through a gate. Turn left to cross a footbridge over the Tavy, and at the junction on the other side turn right (signposted to Peter Tavy again). Go through another gate and follow the path between hedges. It soon joins a surfaced track and after a while the tower of Peter Tavy church comes into view. You pass the Peter Tavy Inn and come out at the main lane through the village.

21. North Brentor to Lydford

Start and finish: Lydford. Grid ref. 510848.

Parking: There is a public car park opposite the Castle Inn towards the southern end of Lydford.

Length: 9.5km (6 miles)

Approximate time: 3 hours

Degree of difficulty: A

Refreshments: The Castle Inn, opposite the car park, is a lovely old inn, with a small, cosy bar, an attractive restaurant and a pretty garden at the back, offering a wide range of food. In the restaurant is a display of coins from the tenth and eleventh centuries, when Lydford was an important administrative centre and the site of the royal mint. About 400 metres/$\frac{1}{4}$ mile to the south is the National Trust's tearoom at Lydford Gorge.

Route summary: Lovely, cool woods and open moorland are the main features of this delightfully varied route. An added bonus is the spectacular views. The outward leg takes you through the pretty Ingo Brake to the moor and round to the slopes of Gibbet Hill. You join the Dartmoor Way just outside North Brentor and follow it back along a track and a road to Lydford. There is very little climbing apart from one stretch at the end. **Note:** The route described skirts the Willsworthy military range, but if you are inclined to go further onto the moor you should telephone 0800 4584868 to find out the times of firing. Do not venture beyond the red and white poles and notice-boards if there are red flags flying from the nearby tors or hills.

Turn right as you leave the car park and, after about 200 metres, turn right again down Silver Street. You now get a very good view ahead to the moor. When the road ends, go straight on along a track. At the junction after a short distance turn right (signposted to Beardon). This is the Lychway, an ancient transmoor route. The whole of Dartmoor Forest is part of the parish of Lydford, and until the thirteenth century everyone within the forest had to take their dead to Lydford Church for burial - a very long journey for the poor folk of the eastern moor. The Lychway was the route they followed. In 1260 Bishop Branscombe of Exeter took pity on them and allowed them to use Widecombe church, but the path continued to be used as a transmoor route.

The track enters Ingo Brake and swings left under a rather splendid railway viaduct; you will find the River Lyd below you on the right. You pass a house and at the end of the track bear right down a path. Cross a footbridge and turn left immediately on the other side (do not go through the gate straight ahead). Go through another gate to leave the wood, and where the path forks go left to a stile. Keep to the left of a field to another stile and then another footbridge. Keep to the left again and then follow the path as it climbs away from the river to a gate. When you come to a track, bear left and go through another gate and then a third. The track takes you to the main A386; turn right.

Follow the road for about 250 metres to a turning on the left; turn off and go through a gateway onto a lane. At the end you go through a gate onto the open moor. Turn right on a track alongside a wall to avoid the military firing range. When the wall turns right, go straight on along the track. After about 100 metres you will find a path going right, off the track, to meet another wall coming in from the right. Cross a stream along the way and then follow the wall. When it turns right, you will find three tracks ahead; one goes straight on, one goes half right and one goes right. Take the middle one. You now get a superb view ahead, with Bodmin Moor visible in the distance on a clear day, and another one to the right over North Devon. Cross a surfaced track and continue to another, unsurfaced one. Cross that to a path. You now have the distinctive shape of Brent Tor, with its church perched on top, half right.

About 600 metres after crossing the second track you will come to another one, this time less clear. Join it and bear right towards two gates you can see, one on each side of the A386; there are a couple of posts to indicate the route. Go down to a kissing-gate, cross the road and go through another kissing-gate on the other side. Follow the path straight ahead to cross a track. When you come to another track, bear right. There are several paths leading off, but you

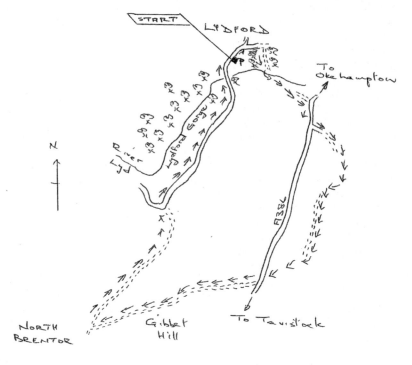

81

LYDFORD CASTLE

should keep to the main track, aiming just to the right of Brent Tor. Do not worry if you go slightly wrong; if you end up too far to the left, you can always correct for any deviation later on. This track leads you round the slopes of Gibbet Hill and comes out at a very clear gravel track. (If you have gone too far to the left, there are plenty of paths to take you down into the valley at this point.)

    * Turn sharp right onto the track. You are now on the Dartmoor Way. After 800 metres/¹/₂ mile you will see a grass track bearing right, marked with a cycle trail sign and the West Devon Way waymark; take that. After another 800 metres/¹/₂ mile you will come to a gate on the left with the West Devon Way waymark on the gatepost. Go through this onto a track, which takes you onto a road. Turn right and follow the road for about 1.5km/1 mile back to Lydford, passing the main entrance to Lydford Gorge and with a good view of the moor to your right. If you would rather avoid this stretch of road walking, you can turn left at the road to reach the Waterfall Entrance to the National Trust's spectacular Lydford Gorge (there is a fee for non-members) and walk up the gorge. This is not actually part of the Dartmoor Way and there is only access from this entrance during the summer, but the gorge is quite superb.

    When you reach the town, you pass first the church and then Lydford Castle. This was never really a castle. Built in the twelfth century, it was the seat of the stannary and forest courts, which heard cases under laws regulating the tin industry and Dartmoor Forest. The basement served as a prison; it had no windows and the only access was via a ladder. It is an interesting site to visit. Just beyond the castle is the car park.

22. Lydford to Bridestowe

THE WAR MEMORIAL,
LYDFORD

Start and finish: Lydford. Grid ref. 510848.

Parking: There is a public car park opposite the Castle Inn towards the southern end of Lydford.

Length: 11.5km (7 miles)

Approximate time: 4 hours

Degree of difficulty: A/B

Refreshments: The Castle Inn is immediately opposite the start of the walk (see previous walk). If you would like a break halfway through, there are two pubs in Bridestowe, the Royal Oak and the White Hart.

Route summary: This is a very varied walk, with some lovely wooded stretches and some excellent views. The outward leg follows the Dartmoor Way, mainly along green lanes and tracks, to its junction with another long-distance route, the Two Castles Trail, just outside Bridestowe. You then return through Bridestowe and along quiet lanes, including a pretty woodland stretch. It is generally fairly easy, although there are a couple of steady climbs in the middle.

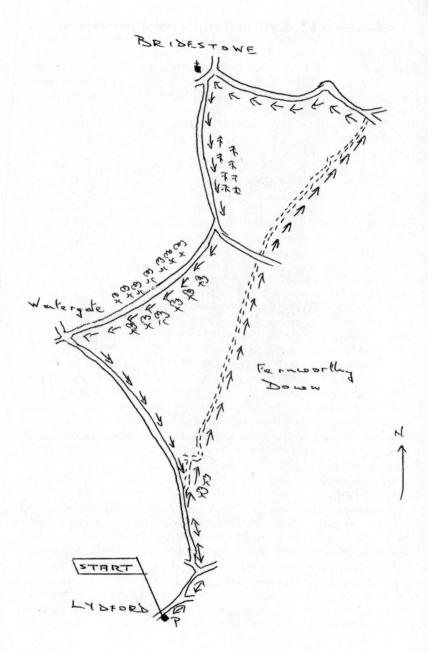

BRIDESTOWE

Watergate

Fernworthy Down

N

START

LYDFORD

* Turn right from the car park and follow the road through Lydford for about 400 metres/¹/₄ mile until you come to the war memorial. Turn left here (signposted to Coryton), then after a few metres right (signposted to Watergate). You pass a campsite on the left and then a group of houses on the right. Just beyond the last house turn right down a rocky green lane, following the public byway sign. This descends gently through a wood for 400 metres/¹/₄ mile to a track. Turn right, following the public byway sign again. Go through a gate and follow the track on the other side to the left to cross a stream. It then climbs gently across Fernworthy Down. At the top you get some wonderful views all around.

After 800 metres/¹/₂ mile you come to the end of the down and go through a gate. At the junction on the other side go straight on, following the West Devon Way waymark. This is a very pleasant broad track lined with trees. After another 800 metres/¹/₂ mile you come to a lane; cross over to another broad track, following the public byway sign. Through the gateways on the right you get a lovely view across to Dartmoor. The track descends to a small clapper bridge alongside a ford. Just beyond it bear left to another clapper bridge to avoid another ford. Turn right on the other side to continue along the track. It climbs gently to a lane; turn left. You now get another good view of the West Devon countryside ahead. At the T-junction after a few metres turn left, following the West Devon Way waymark. After another 400 metres/¹/₄ mile the lane swings sharp left. This is where you leave the Dartmoor Way and join the Two Castles Trail, which links the castles of Okehampton and Launceston. *

Follow this lane, which rejoices in the name Pig's Leg Lane, down to the pretty village of Bridestowe. At the T-junction opposite the church turn left (signposted to Tavistock), and at the next junction follow the main road round to the left (signposted to Tavistock again). The road climbs steadily out of the village, passing a wood on the left. After about 1.2km/³/₄ mile there is a junction; turn right along a lane (signposted to Coryton). It takes you through a lovely wood and descends to the hamlet of Watergate. At the crossroads at the bottom turn left (signposted to Lydford).

You cross a stream and the lane starts to climb steadily. When it levels off, you are rewarded by some excellent views on either side. It then climbs some more and, at the top, goes through a small stretch of woodland. About 1.8km/1 mile after leaving Watergate you will pass the green lane you went out on, on the left. Carry straight on along the lane for 400 metres/¹/₄ mile to the T-junction; turn left and at the war memorial right to return to Lydford and the car park.

23. Bridestowe to Meldon

Start and finish: Bridestowe. Grid ref. 514893.
Parking: In the roads through Bridestowe.
Length: 11.5km (7 miles)
Approximate time: 4 hours
Degree of difficulty: A/B
Refreshments: There are two pubs in Bridestowe. I like the White Hart, a welcoming seventeenth-century coaching inn with a cosy bar, an attractive restaurant and tables outside where you can sit in the sun and watch the village go about its business. They offer a good range of food, from snacks to main meals. If you would like to stop along the way, you pass the unusual Highwayman Inn at Sourton on both the outward and the return legs.
Route summary: This is a relatively easy route, with just one climb up to the moor on the outward leg. The Dartmoor Way takes farm paths to the hamlet of Sourton, where it joins a moorland track to curve round the lower slopes of Sourton Tors, with outstanding views to the west and north (on a clear day you can see both Bodmin Moor and Exmoor). A green lane then takes you down to Meldon, another little hamlet. There you leave the Way and join a disused railway line, now a cycle track, to return to Sourton. More farm paths and a road bring you back to Bridestowe.

The walk starts outside the churchyard; take the road immediately opposite, with the school on the right and the Royal Oak on the left. Follow it as it winds and climbs out of the village. You immediately get a good view ahead to Dartmoor.

 * After 1km/³⁄₄ mile, as the lane turns right, leave it to bear left across a ladder stile, following the public footpath sign and the West Devon Way and Two Castles Trail waymarks. Keep to the right of three fields separated by stiles, with a good view of Sourton Tors ahead. Follow the path straight across the fourth field to a gap in a bank and bear left on the other side to another stile. Keep to the right of two more fields. There is another stile in the far right-hand corner of the second; cross it and keep to the left on the other side. Cross a track to yet another stile and keep to the left again. Go through a gate onto a track and follow it behind some houses until you see a gate on your right. Go through it and up a track to the left. This brings you to the A386 at Sourton.

Cross the road and turn left along the footpath on the other side. Follow it for about 300 metres to a surfaced track opposite the Highwayman Inn (signposted as a bridlepath to the moor). Turn up here and follow the track as it becomes rougher and climbs past a church. Cross a bridge over a disused railway line, heading straight towards Sourton Tors. Go through a gate and follow the track as it climbs straight ahead alongside the left-hand wall. When

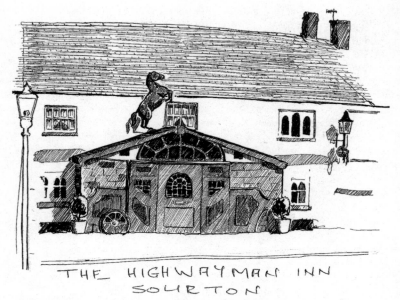

THE HIGHWAYMAN INN
SOURTON

the wall turns left, go straight on for another 100 metres to a junction; turn left along a slightly narrower track through the bracken. You now have a wonderful view to your left, with Bodmin Moor visible in the distance on a clear day, and an equally good one ahead to North Devon.

Cross another grassy track and continue as the one you are on curves right. As you do so, you will be able to see Exmoor in the distance ahead of you if the visibility is good. About 800 metres/¹/₂ mile after joining this track the bracken around you will clear and you will find a wall ahead of you. Turn left, go through a gap in a low wall and follow the wall on your right. You pass a bridlepath sign pointing to Meldon and Meldon Reservoir, but it is some distance from the junction where you have to turn. You now get a good view on the right across the West Okement River to Yes Tor. When the wall curves left, follow it round to a gate. Follow the track on the other side between two walls. Go through a gate into a field. Towards the end there is a path junction; go straight on through a gate into a green lane, following the sign to Meldon. After 800 metres/¹/₂ mile the green lane joins a surfaced lane; go straight on for about 300 metres until the lane goes under a bridge. *

This is where you leave the Dartmoor Way. Just before the bridge go left up a surfaced track to a disused railway line; turn left. This is a lovely track: easy to walk along and fringed with hedgerows filled with wild flowers and birds. After about 1.5km/1 mile you will come to a bridge with a path going left. Do not take it, but continue under the bridge. After another 400 metres/¹/₄ mile the line crosses a surfaced track, and 800 metres/¹/₂ mile beyond that it goes under Lavis Bridge. Another 300 metres brings you to Sourton, and you will find the churchyard on your right and a bridge ahead. Turn right off the disused railway here and go through a gate and down the track you came out on, back to the A386.

Turn left and follow it for 150 metres to Windard Terrace on the right. Turn down there, and at the end of the surfaced road take the grassy track on the left to a gate. Keep to the left of the field on the other side to another gate. Keep to the left again to a third gate. In the far left-hand corner of the next field is another gate; go through that and follow the path to yet another gate. Follow the hedge on the other side round to the left. Go through a gateway and keep left again to go through a gap halfway along the bank ahead of you. Go straight across the next field to a gate and stile. Bear right on the other side to another gate. Turn left on the other side and, after a few metres, right across a footbridge to a track. Follow it to the left and then to the right past a house.

After a few metres you will find a footpath sign on the left; cross a stile and keep to the right of a field to a stile on the right. Bear left on the other side to yet another stile in the far left-hand corner of the field. Cross it and climb some steps to a road. Turn left; there is a surfaced path, first on the right-hand side and then on the left. After 600 metres turn left down a path and a road, and follow the road back to Bridestowe.

24. Meldon to Okehampton

Start and finish: Meldon Reservoir. Grid ref. 561917.
Parking: In the reservoir car park.
Length: 10km (6¼ miles)
Approximate time: 3½ hours
Degree of difficulty: C
Refreshments: There are no refreshments at the start of the walk, but there are several pubs, restaurants and cafés in Okehampton, halfway round. See Walk 1.

Route summary: This is a superb walk, with a variety of scenery and perhaps the best views on Dartmoor. The Dartmoor Way along here goes through two lovely woods alongside the West Okement River, one at Meldon and the other at Okehampton. The return leg takes you through another wood to Okehampton Camp and back across the moor, with views that on a clear day take in three moors: Dartmoor, Bodmin Moor and Exmoor. There is some steep climbing as you leave Okehampton, but once on the open moor the going is easy. **Note:** The route described skirts the Okehampton military range, but if you are inclined to go further onto the moor you should telephone 0800 4584868 to find out the times of firing. Do not venture beyond the red and white poles and noticeboards if there are red flags flying from the nearby tors or hills.

Turn right out of the car park and follow the lane back. To the right you can see the moor stretching into the distance, with Meldon Quarry in the foreground. After 600 metres you will come to a T-junction; turn right.

* This is the start of this leg of the Dartmoor Way. Go under a railway bridge and after 250 metres, just beyond a row of white cottages, turn right along a track. Pass the village hall and continue along the track to a farm. You will be faced with three gates; take the one straight ahead onto a green lane. It swings to the right and, just after it does so, turn left, following the public footpath sign and the West Devon Way waymark. Follow the path through a gate into Meldon Wood. You can hear the West Okement River down on your right, and from time to time you will see it through the trees. The path descends to it. Cross a footbridge and turn left on the other side.

This is a particularly beautiful stretch, with the river cascading over the rocks on your left and the pretty, peaceful wood all around. After a few hundred metres, however, you will hear the traffic on the A30 ahead. The path turns away from the river. At the junction go straight on, parallel to the road, to a parking area. Cross it to a road and turn left. Follow the road across the A30, and on the other side turn right along a track, following the public bridlepath sign, and cross a cattle grid. After 500 metres the track ends at a farm. Go round to the right to a gate, following the blue bridlepath waymark, and turn left to follow a fence. This leads you to a rough track on the other side of the farmyard. It becomes less clear, but you should keep to the fence on the left. At the path junction go straight on.

Go through a gate at the end of the field and onto a golf course. Cross a track and follow the path across the course, which is marked with red lines on both sides. The path joins a track, and the ruins of Okehampton Castle appear half left. Now in the hands of English Heritage, this castle was built to protect the route to Cornwall, and was once the home of the Earls of Devon. It is a very atmospheric site, and well worth a visit if you have the time. At the fork by the clubhouse take the main track to the left to a lane. Cross a cattle grid and enter a wood.

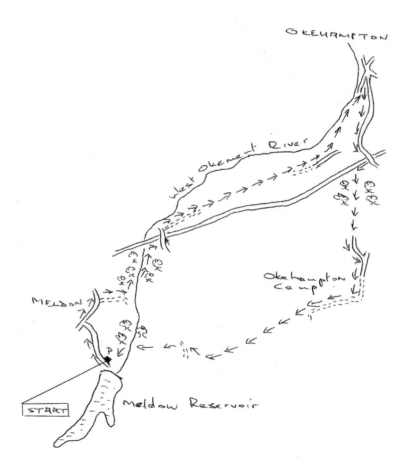

OKEHAMPTON
CASTLE

After a few hundred metres you will see a path on the left, signposted to Okehampton Castle. Take that and follow it down through the wood to rejoin the West Okement. At the bottom you will find a footbridge; cross it if you want to visit the castle, but otherwise carry straight on to a kissing-gate. Follow the path on the other side, alongside the river. You pass a hospital and join a road; carry straight on, and after 300 metres you will come to the centre of Okehampton and the end of this leg of the Dartmoor Way. *

Turn right at the T-junction and immediately right again, following the sign for the camp. This road climbs through the outskirts of the town. When you come to the junction with Station Road, go straight on (signposted to the camp again). It is a long and steady climb of about 800 metres/¹/₂ mile. Towards the top the road swings left to cross a railway line and then right to cross the A30. On the other side turn right down a surfaced track, following the public footpath sign. When you are faced by a gate, follow the track to the left. The surfacing ends and you enter a wood. At the fork after a few metres, just before a house, go right to a stile. On the other side leave the track and turn left, following the sign for Okehampton Camp.

You cross a track and climb steeply through the wood. After a while it gives way to open moorland, but you continue to climb. Now, however, you can look back for a superb view across to North Devon and, on a clear day, to Exmoor. When you get to the top, you will see Okehampton Camp ahead

92

of you, with the moors beyond. Cross to a cattle grid into the camp. On the other side take the road straight ahead, following the black arrow. At the top go left, following the black arrow and the path sign. When you come to a T-junction, turn right, still following the black arrow and the path sign. This road takes you to a rough track and a stile. Cross the field on the other side, with an excellent view of a trio of tors ahead of you: Rowtor, West Mill Tor and Yes Tor.

Cross another stile onto the open moor and turn right along a track, which follows the line of the wall. You now have superb views to the right to North Devon and to the left over Dartmoor. After 400 metres/¼ mile the track turns left; leave it to go straight on, following the wall. After a while another outstanding panorama comes into view ahead, across West Devon to the third moor you can see on a clear day - Bodmin Moor - and Sourton Tors half left. About 1.2km/¾ mile after leaving the track, the wall swings sharp right; follow it round.

You will now see the impressive Meldon Viaduct ahead of you as you go down a steep hill to a gate onto a track. Turn left and go through another gate. Just before you come to a hut, turn right along a broad path into a valley. When you get there, you will see the wall of Meldon Reservoir on the left. Turn right along another broad path, which will take you to a footbridge across the West Okement. Cross it into a wood and turn left on the other side. After a while you will leave the wood and climb across some open moorland to a gate onto a road. Turn right and after a couple of metres right again through another gate to the car park.

Index